Warning Analysis for the Information Age: *Rethinking the Intelligence Process*

by John W. Bodnar

Center for Strategic Intelligence Research
Joint Military Intelligence College

WASHINGTON, DC
December 2003

The Joint Military Intelligence College supports and encourages research on intelligence issues that distills lessons and improves support to policy-level and operational consumers

Warning Analysis for the Information Age: Rethinking the Intelligence Process, by John W. Bodnar

This book bequeaths to the Defense Intelligence Agency, and to the Intelligence Community at large, a substantiated vision, with examples, of how analysts can exploit already-available, massive databases to tackle many of the most vexing problems that we face. Dr. Bodnar builds on the earlier work and insight of Cynthia Grabo, whose book *Anticipating Surprise: Analysis for Strategic Warning* was recently published by the Joint Military Intelligence College's Center for Strategic Intelligence Research. The author also usefully integrates into this book the often-cited but rarely-seen original work of the USAF's strategic and operational philosopher Colonel John Boyd. Together with the accompanying, classified case studies that are available to the Community on Intelink, this book reaches farther than any other toward the objective of bringing together substantive expertise with an accessible, methodologically sound analytical strategy in the service of the U.S. Intelligence Community. Those who go on to apply this method will not only derive fresh understanding from existing data, but will also be able to guide future intelligence collection in an appropriately frugal fashion.

Russell.Swenson@dia.mil, Editor

Library of Congress Control Number 2003114408
ISBN 0-9656195-8-3

ACKNOWLEDGEMENTS

The author gratefully acknowledges the following individuals, who reviewed and commented on early drafts of this book.

Jim Murphy and Kelcy Allwein of the Defense Intelligence Agency; Kim McVaney of the National Security Agency, Mike Maskelaris of MITRE Corporation, and Frank Hughes, faculty member at the Joint Military Intelligence College.

In addition, several individuals provided invaluable assistance or advice on the classified case studies.

From the Defense Intelligence Agency: Dr. Eric Hehl, CW3 David Temby, Mary Highsmith, and CDR James van der Velde.

From the Joint Military Intelligence College: LTC Jeffrey Johnson, JMIC student; Dr. William Williamson, faculty member; and Research Fellow colleague Rebecca Katz.

CONTENTS

COMMENTARIES

Warning Analysis For The Information Age: Rethinking The Intelligence Process

JEFFREY R. COOPER*

Looking toward the challenges posed to the Intelligence Community by the changed strategic circumstances of the Information Age, Dr. Bodnar, an experienced intelligence analyst with a deep technical background, weaves together four themes in addressing the emerging demands of warning intelligence. The important core theme is the utility of his Multidimensional Analysis (MDA) methodology in confronting the complexity of Information-Age warning challenges, an analytic approach he developed while working on a variety of problems posed by foreign development of weapons of mass destruction. The second theme builds on Cynthia Grabo's recently republished classic *Handbook of Warning Intelligence* and tunes those lessons for Information-Age rather than Industrial-Age conditions. Bodnar's third theme is to highlight the utility of Col. John Boyd's theory of the OODA-loop decision cycle and integrate it into the warning analysis framework. Finally, from his perspective as a working analyst, Bodnar provides, in a series of suggestions on fixing analytical and resource constraints, a strategy to improve intelligence analysis. To this interesting and useful work, I would offer several thoughts for additional emphases.

OVERALL COMMENTS

Properly in my view, Bodnar, in concert with many observers,[1] sees the Information Age as signifying a fundamental shift away from a deterministic and linear Newtonian paradigm to a complex adaptive systems perspective grounded in non-linearity and modern, quantum physics. Bodnar integrates this "paradigm shift" theme throughout his paper; however, perhaps in keeping with his scientific background and in focusing narrowly on the analytical issues, he fails to fully

*Corporate Vice-President for Technology and Chief Scientist, Science Applications International Corporation Strategies Group.

[1]See, for example, David S. Alberts and Thomas J. Czerwinski, eds., *Complexity, Global Politics, and National Security* (Washington, DC: National Defense University Press, June 1997).

appreciate other distinctive elements of that Industrial-Age model, besides the deterministic Newtonian linearity, that are now also changing and contributing to our emerging warning problems.

Industrial-Age powers drew their strength from three underlying and interrelated roots: political, economic, and technological. First, building upon the post-Westphalian emergence of nationalism, these nation-states drew legitimacy and political strength from large cohesive publics, which could also provide sizable military forces. Second, industrialization and mass production fueled rapid economic growth that together allowed these nation-states to field and support very large military forces. Third, new technologies provided large-scale mobility and immensely lethal firepower for these forces, enabling offensive military operations at a distance. The potency of scale dominated the sources of national power, but the Industrial Age required efficient organizations and processes to harness and exploit this power. Thus, the importance of Weber's hierarchical bureaucracies that brought professionalization, specialization and routinization to management. Also, Taylor's application of standardized and systematized processes to manufacturing cannot be overemphasized as key elements of the Industrial-Age paradigm that demanded the ability to predict and control these mass-scale entities.

Throughout the Industrial Age, these same factors—mass, standardization, and predictability—also underwrote the sources of military strength and shaped strategies and operational approaches to warfare. But those very qualities also enabled us to adopt and exploit a warning paradigm based on assumptions (such as mass and linearity) that danger would come from large-scale activities. These threats, almost by definition, would be visible—and deterministically predictable—if we could access their signatures. The Information Age has changed these comfortable assumptions about the tractability of providing warning based on observable activities and predictable processes; new threats may come in very small packages that are difficult to detect, or subtle activities with non-linear consequences that are hard to observe. While I might disagree with Bodnar as to the magnitude of the threat posed by many of these new challenges (especially as compared with tens of thousands of nuclear weapons wielded with deadly malice), I certainly agree that this new environment is more challenging, with respect to knowability (in the formal sense), observability, and predictability if we continue to rely on our inherited tools and practices. Exactly for this reason, I would strengthen Bodnar's implicit call to re-examine issues of analytic process. This will demand returning to first-order issues of both phenomenology and epistemology.

A second area that I would emphasize is the diversity of the new warning challenges. First, I would emend Bodnar's definitions of warning. All intelligence informs decisionmakers; but warning intelligence is distinctive because it must be intended to trigger action by the decisionmaker. Strategic warning intelligence especially must concern itself not just that a nation (or other group) may hold hostile intentions and be acquiring appropriate capabilities to serve them, but also that other changes—such as new technologies, political institutions or dynamics, economic dislocations, or challenges to human security such as disease or environmental catastrophe, could pose fundamental challenges to U.S. interests or policies. I would also add Operational Warning to his categorization.

Tactical Warning (TW) is an alert; it should denote that the activity of concern (such as a surprise attack) is immediately imminent or unfortunately underway. It should be specific with respect to at least *where* and *when*, even it cannot answer *who* and *how*. As Bodnar correctly notes, response to TW is immediate and must be with resources and plans at hand. Strategic Warning (SW) should identify the existence of a potential threat, either in terms of intention or capability, and provide sufficient time for policymakers to assimilate, plan, and provide resources for offsetting responses, as Bodnar recognizes. Operational Warning is the essential link between these two; it both alerts that the adversary is preparing to embark upon his inimical activity and identifies its particular character. It provides the necessary time to mobilize and activate the response, as well as to trigger close monitoring of the indicators for TW. As an example, appropriate Strategic Warning in the mid-1990s would have alerted that Islamic Fundamentalism was becoming a strategic threat to U.S. global interests. Operational Warning would have cued that both Al-Qaeda and "airplanes as bombs" were instrumentalities of particular concern. Tactical Warning would have provided notice of imminent attack. The warning failure of 9/11 was not merely the lack of Tactical Warning, but Operational and Strategic as well.

In the MDA, Bodnar provides a six-dimensional methodology that is very structured, but inherently flexible in terms of the particular analytic tools and models that can be incorporated. It is gratifying that he also appreciates how limited the evidence-driven "connect the dots" model is in its applicability and that employing other models that rely more on hypothesis generation and testing are essential. Moreover, although Bodnar lives within an "evidence-based culture," he stresses the need to provide context as the only way to ensure that the evidence can be interpreted correctly; "the facts" don't speak for themselves. In particular, he highlights the need to adopt recursive hypothesis generation and testing protocols to ensure that anomalous information is not simply ignored or drowned by masses of confirmatory evidence fed in streams enriched as an inadvertent by-product of a filtering process based on "*a priori* relevance" determinations.

In addition to his promoting the inherent strengths of the MDA methodology, Bodnar is particularly strong in making useful suggestions on improving other analytic processes in intelligence by adopting similarly structured practices more akin to scientific research than to the humanities.

Other Specific Comments

By highlighting MDA only within the context of warning intelligence, Bodnar significantly shortchanges its potential utility to address other serious intelligence analysis shortfalls. As one element of his fourth theme, he recognizes the pervasive adverse impacts of emphasizing current intelligence over assessments and estimative intelligence—including in-depth warning analysis—but he fails to suggest explicitly that such structured, multi-element analytic procedures could also improve many other types of intelligence efforts as a corrective to the reportorial character of current intelligence.

Although focused on improving warning intelligence, Bodnar touches lightly on a number of other existing problems that impede good intelligence analysis overall. He usefully suggests that a multi-step analytic process include a systematic examination of how we model the adversary and conduct the entire analysis process. The frequent and advised references to "tradecraft" in community writings recognize the continuing craft character of the intelligence enterprise, despite the trappings of advanced technologies. One little-understood consequence of the craft culture, however, is the evolutionary and accreted nature of analytic practices and habits—especially those that proved successful in the past; a second is the relative lack of systematic examination of these analytic processes and the epistemology that underlies them. In an era of rapid and significant change, a craft culture may not be able to adapt sufficiently quickly to meet the new challenges. Moreover, in a craft culture, much critical domain expertise and process information (as well as standards, values, and *élan*) often remains tacit and embodied in human expertise—or in individual analyst's "shoeboxes"—rather than instantiated in structured, catalogued and retrievable form accessible to others. He highlights the importance of addressing this issue before that expertise is lost forever.

Bodnar recognizes that waiting on customer requests to build the in-depth analytic base necessary to MDA, as well as to other intelligence efforts, may not provide sufficient time to do the job properly when the need for good answers becomes pressing. In doing so, he implicitly raises the key issue of how the IC can be more proactive and go beyond the formal customer-driven requirements process. Bodnar also recognizes that despite the customer's usual interest in "an answer," not all "stories" are linear; he recognizes that telling the correct story in a manner that ensures the listener truly understands the message is essential. He also exposes the serious issue that while very substantial resources have been invested in the IC's information infrastructure, relatively little has been spent on tools to enhance the individual analyst's cognitive performance—especially among all-source analysts, or to effectively support endemic work practices such as "shoeboxes."

ADDITIONAL COMMENTARIES:
Warning Analysis For The Information Age: Rethinking The Intelligence Process

Dr. Norman Kahn*

Dr. Bodnar's work identifies and integrates a number of elements critical to the Intelligence Community's understanding of efforts on the part of both state and non-state actors to develop weapons of mass destruction. Specifically, he identifies human sources, signals intelligence, and open-source exploitation as key factors; and he develops a potent argument for integrating information on people, places and programs and making this information available to the intelligence analyst in the form of automated relational databases. This approach, which he defines as "multidimensional analysis," is already in use by savvy analysts. Its widespread acceptance clearly will enhance the Community's ability to provide deeper and more sophisticated input to policymakers who bear the ultimate responsibility of responding to national security threats.

F. J. Hughes**

We are indeed at the threshold of a paradigm shift in intelligence analysis. The research work of the Advanced Research Development Activity (ARDA), an Intelligence-Community-wide effort, is seeking to define how we should advance our strategies, operational concepts, and organizations in a fashion corresponding to Dr. Bodnar's vision. ARDA brings a potent dynamic into play that focuses on Discovery, Exploitation, and Analysis of intelligence information. Bodnar is a harbinger of a powerful shift in thinking that can shape the future of intelligence in a world that has changed dramatically. His work represents a significant step forward in intelligence studies and serves as an invaluable reference for tomorrow's intelligence analysts who confront the task of implementing complex judgmental analysis.

---

*Program Manager, Bio-Defense Programs, Intelligence Technology Innovation Center.

**Faculty Member, Joint Military Intelligence College.

Chapter 1

STRATEGIC WARNING IN A WORLD OF WEAPONS OF MASS DESTRUCTION (WMD) AND TERRORISM

John W. Bodnar, PhD

Changes in technology in the past half century have destroyed the ability to provide warning intelligence by traditional means. How can new technologies facilitate new methodologies to provide warning intelligence in the Information Age?

Sputnik, 9/11, and the End of Warning Intelligence

The 9/11 attacks made very clear that the concept of warning intelligence has totally changed. I suggest that the ability to provide warning intelligence was not very different up to the beginning of World War II from what it was in prehistoric times, but the changes in technology during that war began a new age of intelligence. To understand these changes and their effects, to start with, we need a definition of warning; I suggest:

- **Tactical Warning** — warning of potential actions by an adversary to which a response can be mounted with current resources.
- **Strategic Warning** — warning of potential actions by an adversary for which a response will require a significant reallocation of resources.

The aim of warning intelligence is to be able to provide warfighters and policymakers with specific indicators of the potential actions of the adversary. We also need to realize that most of the intelligence we do is not warning but rather current intelligence. Current Intelligence is matching recently collected intelligence against warning indicators to be able to predict the next actions of the adversary.

Every society has a need to provide resources both for its defense—"guns"—and for its sustaining infrastructure or economy—"butter." A best-case scenario for a society would be an environment where it did not have to provide for defense so it could allocate all its resources toward its economy, but, with the possible exception of some remote Pacific islands, societies have always had to reallocate at least some of their resources toward a military. The next-best scenario is for a society to allocate virtually all its resources to "butter" and only build "guns" when attack from without is imminent. A society that can have "butter now" to build a strong economy but only build "guns later" when it sees an imminent attack will be, in the long run, stronger than a society that needs a standing military.

A "butter-now-guns-later" strategy depends on strategic warning. A wholesale change from a peacetime economy to a wartime economy requires time, and if intelligence is not available and used for a national-level policy change, the nation will find itself with only "butter" and some half-built "guns" in the face of a fully armed opponent.

The Roman Empire survived for centuries in part because it could provide effective strategic warning. Since Roman-era intelligence could travel only as fast as military forces that might be on the move, it was not unheard-of that a force of a hundred thousand Persians could come over the hill toward a village on the frontiers of the Roman Empire without any prior warning. This lack of tactical warning meant that the forces immediately at hand would be overrun, but while that occurred, warning could be passed throughout the Empire. This strategic warning would then allow a reallocation of assets to meet the threat: either a massing of legions from far-flung areas along the well-maintained roads; or a call up or arming of troops from the populace of the neighboring regions. The ability to reallocate standing forces or change from "butter" to "guns" meant that the price paid in taxes across the Empire was considered small in contrast to the security afforded by the Empire.

In contrast, the nations of nineteenth century Europe could not employ a "butter-now-guns-later" strategy because an invading army could go through the entire nation before there was any hope of raising a military force from scratch. In that era, warning intelligence required collection inside other nations to follow their military buildup. This led to the presence of standing armies across Europe—a "both guns and butter" strategy—by which every nation attempted to have a tactical warning capability to spark the call up of a large enough force, instantly, to repel the attacks.

The Information Age and the End of Warning Intelligence

Up through World War II the United States had the ability to provide strategic warning in a way similar to that of the Roman Empire. In the absence of any national threats in the Americas, the navy on the oceans surrounding the U.S. provided a "tripwire" in much the same way as the Roman legions on the frontiers of the Empire. Once in place, this system then only needed to use current intelligence to mobilize the proper response to a threat. This provided the U.S. with the ability to employ a "butter-now-guns-later" strategy where it could maintain a primarily civilian economy but only mobilize in times of national threat. In this sense, Pearl Harbor was a tactical surprise but not a strategic surprise. The attack caused massive local damage and destruction to the Pacific fleet, but due to the size of the Pacific Ocean the attack itself served as strategic warning in that it gave the U.S. a "wakeup call" to change from "butter" to "guns" with plenty of time to meet the expanding Japanese and Axis threat.

In spite of a huge tactical surprise at Pearl Harbor, the U.S. homeland was never in significant danger because the U.S. has the ability to change very rapidly from an inward-looking civilian economy to an outward-looking military juggernaut. The vast expanse of oceans surrounding the U.S. meant that strategic warning was not very hard. Strategic warning always implied threats that were distant—either in space or time. But that changed markedly twice in the lifetimes of those who remember Pearl Harbor—as space and time "shrank" as the world entered the Information Age. For the U.S., not only strategic warning but even tactical warning virtually disappeared.

The first blow to the U.S.'s ability to provide warning intelligence came with the launch of Sputnik. As soon as the Soviet Union had the technical capability to build and employ targetable, nuclear-tipped ICBM's, the world instantly shrank to the functional equivalent of eighteenth-century Europe. The U.S. could be threatened by a military force that could be built virtually unseen inside the Soviet Union and employed with only minutes' worth of warning. This meant that the U.S. could no longer think "butter-now-guns-later" and led to an arms race reminiscent of those involving England, France, Prussia, and Austria in the 1800s, where standing armies were the order of the day. Even though the Soviet Union was half-a-world away, it was only twenty minutes away as the missile flies over the North Pole. The coupling of WMD with long-range delivery systems, in the form of missiles tipped with nuclear warheads, changed warfare and warning intelligence forever.

In the world of WMD, our "strategic weapons" and "Strategic Air Force" really only could have tactical warning—the ability to respond *now* with resources currently available. This was a wakeup call for the U.S. because strategic warning, as we had previously known it, was gone. In the Cold War, tactical warning was possible by monitoring missile silos and military movements by satellite. But true strategic warning was gone. The U.S. now needed to maintain a large, standing military for the first time in its history—a shift from a "butter-now-guns-later" strategy to a much costlier "both-guns-and-butter" strategy.

The second blow to the U.S. ability to provide warning intelligence came on 11 September 2001. Terrorist attacks from within the U.S. itself directed by terrorist groups half-a-world away meant that time had shrunk after 9/11 just as space had shrunk after Sputnik. In this case the wakeup call was the realization that tactical warning, as it has always been defined, was also gone. Tactical warning always depended on monitoring the movements of opposing military forces and deploying current assets to meet the threat. But what if the threat was U.S. persons using U.S. assets within the continental U.S.? The very foundation of even tactical warning was shattered in a world where an attack ordered anywhere in the world could come virtually anywhere, anytime, with assets that were themselves peaceful only minutes before.

Additionally, in the Information Age the concept of a nation-state has blurred to where multi-national corporations and agencies sometimes are as powerful as the nations in which they operate. Therefore, in a world of non-national terrorist organizations and alliances that can shift between religious and political affiliates, collecting intelligence on a state may often be misleading or irrelevant unless it is integrated with intelligence on that state's interactions not only with other countries but multi-national corporations and organizations as well.

For the U.S., the post-9/11 world in the dawn of the Information Age is more different from the Industrial-Age world of Pearl Harbor than world of Pearl Harbor was different from the world of the Roman Empire.

In the Information Age, the Intelligence Community (IC) in the U.S. is faced with unprecedented challenges:

- How can it provide strategic warning in a world of WMD where a massive attack from half-a-world away can occur minutes from now?
- How can it provide tactical warning in a world of terrorism where adversaries who looked peaceful minutes ago can attack inside the U.S. minutes from now?

This requires a total rethinking about what we mean by warning intelligence.

Warning Intelligence for the Information Age

In 1972 the Defense Intelligence Agency published Cynthia Grabo's *Handbook of Warning Intelligence*, re-published by the Joint Military Intelligence College in an updated and declassified version in 2002 as *Anticipating Surprise: Analysis for Strategic Warning*. Ms. Grabo laid the groundwork to codify theories on warning intelligence and strategic warning. I aim to build on her thoughts to indicate that warning intelligence at the dawn of the Information Age is as important—or even more important—as it was when she wrote her first manuscript at the height of the Cold War. However, the technological changes that have shrunk the world in both space and time are changing the very nature of intelligence. Therefore, I will draw heavily on Ms. Grabo's thoughts—sometimes to reiterate timeless lessons on warning intelligence and sometimes to indicate the need for an Information-Age addition to her Industrial-Age argument.

> Warning intelligence at the strategic level, or as it is sometimes called "indications intelligence," is largely a post-World War II development. More specifically, it was a product of the early days of the Cold War, when we began to perceive that the Soviet Union and other communist countries were embarked on courses inimical to the interests of the Free World and which could lead to surprise actions or open aggression. Enemy actions in World War II, such as the Japanese attack on Pearl Harbor in 1941, had dispelled many of the conventional or historical concepts about how wars begin. The fear that America's enemies once again might undertake devastating, surprise military action—and without prior declaration of war or other conventional warning—had become very real. The advent of modern weapons and long-range delivery systems further increased the need for warning to avoid surprise attack.[1]
>
> Cynthia Grabo
> *Anticipating Surprise: Analysis for Strategic Warning*

As indicated by Ms. Grabo above, "warning intelligence" got its start in response to the shattering of the old paradigm for strategic warning, when the oceans could no longer serve as a tripwire. In the past we could afford surprise. While Pearl Harbor was tactically devastating, it was not strategically devastating. Indeed, Admiral Yamamoto, the commander of the Japanese fleet at Pearl Harbor was believed to have realized the strategic mistake in that attack in saying, "We have just roused a sleeping giant." In an age of WMD even tactical surprise is not an allowable option because a single attack with a single biological or nuclear weapon can potentially be worse than multiple Pearl Harbors.

> In an era of asymmetric warfare in which our national security and well being can be seriously threatened by hostile groups as well as nations, it is imperative that lessons from the past not be forgotten but brought up to date and the discipline of warning reinvigorated. Warning intelligence differs significantly from current intelligence and the preparation of long-range estimates. It accepts the presumption of surprise and incomplete

---

[1]Cynthia M. Grabo, *Anticipating Surprise: Analysis for Strategic Warning*, ed. Jan Goldman (Washington DC: Joint Military Intelligence College's Center for Strategic Intelligence Research, 2002), 1. Cited hereafter as Grabo.

intelligence and requires exhaustive research upon which to build the case for specific warning.[2]

LTG James Williams (Ret.), USAF
Former Director, Defense Intelligence Agency

The new Directorate for Analysis will be charged with transforming our analysis from descriptive assessments to complex judgmental analysis required to identify vulnerabilities and provide options for policymakers and warfighters.[3]

VADM Lowell E. Jacoby
Director, Defense Intelligence Agency

Warning-oriented intelligence reflects a compelling need—unprecedented prior to the development of WMD—not to be surprised. By not being surprised, I mean that analysts must be able to provide detailed enough judgments—with supporting reporting—so that both the warfighter and the policymaker can anticipate the actions of potential adversaries and take timely action to support U.S. interests. In short, it is incumbent on the Information-Age analyst to provide both the warfighter and policymaker with options: On the basis of what the adversary has the capability to do, how will he likely act? What actions can we take to stop, change, or respond to those actions, and what are the probable consequences of those actions?

To do this, the Information-Age warning analyst must be able to peer into the future with a level of granularity many times more detailed than ever required before. Rather than providing targeting to the warfighter at the level of which city or military base contains the threat, the Information-age analyst must be able to tell the warfighter which building half-a-world-away contains the nuclear device or BW fermenter so that he can interdict that facility with a single smart bomb or cruise missile with minimal collateral damage. Rather than giving the policymaker broad-brush descriptions of a country's WMD capabilities, the Information-Age analyst must be able to tell the policymaker exactly where that state is procuring the materials to build that nuclear or biological weapon so that he can demarche the shipment of supplies before the weapon can be assembled. If the

---

[2]LTG James Williams (Ret.), USA, Former Director, Defense Intelligence Agency, quoted in Cynthia M. Grabo, *Anticipating Surprise: Analysis for Strategic Warning*, ed. Jan Goldman (Washington DC: Joint Military Intelligence College's Center for Strategic Intelligence Research, 2002), iii.

[3]VADM Lowell E. Jacoby, Director, DIA, as posted on the Director's Intelink home page, February 2003.

Industrial-Age analyst miscounted a single aircraft carrier or tank, that really did not affect the course of the war very much or the policy to reduce the risk of that war; but if the Information-Age analyst assesses that a nation has zero nuclear weapons when they really have one or two, the results could be devastating.

Chapter 2

FROM CURRENT INTELLIGENCE TO WARNING ANALYSIS

A new kind of strategic warning is required for WMD and terrorism. How can we rethink our assumptions on intelligence to redefine methodologies for providing strategic warning?

As the ability to collect intelligence and project power has increased with the massive technological breakthroughs of the past half-century, the pace of the intelligence cycle has increased. This has put a premium on collecting and reporting current intelligence. Cynthia Grabo has argued that current intelligence is different from warning intelligence.

> As intelligence collection becomes more sophisticated, voluminous and expensive, and devices multiply for the rapid reporting and community-wide exchange and display of the latest information, we must take care that we do not lose sight of what warning really is: the considered judgment of the finest analytic minds available, based on an exhaustive and objective review of all available indications, which is conveyed to the policy official in sufficiently convincing language that he is persuaded of its validity and takes appropriate action to protect the national interest.[4]

She further notes that the requirements for current intelligence and warning intelligence are very different in their pace and approach.

> It is possible that the single most prevalent misconception about warning is that the latest information is necessarily the most important, or that warning will be insured (or at least made much more likely) if only collection can be speeded up and information communicated more rapidly to more alert centers. The effects of this type of preoccupation with currency of information are likely to be twofold: long-term, basic intelligence and in-depth analysis tend to suffer both in the allocation of personnel and in prestige; and the cumulative analysis of indications tends to be forgotten in favor of portraying the latest information on charts or display boards in situation rooms. From this, it is but a step to accepting the view that what the adversary is doing this minute is the most important indication of his intentions, or that information which is more than 24 hours old is valueless or at least of minor value to warning.

---

[4] Grabo, 169.

> But this is not strategic warning—and excessive attention to current information tends to obscure the significance of strategic, long-term actions by a potential adversary.[5]

Ms. Grabo's message is clear. By building our organizations to provide current intelligence, we are hampering our ability to provide warning. To see the road ahead, we must force ourselves to think totally opposite from our custom—not to see how *fast* we can produce intelligence but rather how *well* we can produce intelligence. That message was clear for the bipolar world of the Cold War—the need to rethink how we think about intelligence is even more accentuated in the multi-polar world of WMD and terrorism.

> Warning is cumulative, not merely current. Intelligence reporting at all times must take care to insure that the consumer knows the cumulative background and understands that the latest indication is but one of many which in their totality give us insight into what may occur... The best warning analysis is the product of a detailed and continuing review of all information, going back weeks and months, which may be relevant to the current situation, and a solid basic understanding of the potential enemy's objectives, doctrines, practices, and organizations... Most crises have roots going deep into the past, much farther than we usually realize until after they erupt. Preparation for war or possible war often can be traced back for months once it becomes clear that a real threat exists, and pieces of information which appeared questionable, unreliable or even ridiculous when received will suddenly have great relevance to the present situation, provided that the analyst has saved them and can fit them into the current pattern. Further, information which is months old when received (and therefore scarcely current intelligence) may be immensely valuable. An indication is not useless or invalid because it occurred months ago but you just found out about it today; it may demonstrate that the preparations for conflict have been far more extensive and significant than you had believed.[6]

In the Cold War warning intelligence required "going back weeks and months." In the world of WMD and terrorism warning intelligence requires going back "years and decades." In the case of WMD "preparation for conflict" often has started decades before the conflict—at the time a state decides to begin building WMD. In terrorism "preparation for conflict" may have also started

[5]Grabo, 164.
[6]Grabo, 164, 5-6.

decades before the conflict when a superpower has gone home and those fighting that power perceived that it must have turned its enmity toward another foe.

> The term *strategic warning* somewhat regrettably has no single, accepted definition. To those in the world of warning intelligence, strategic warning is generally viewed as relatively long-term, or synonymous with the "earliest possible warning" which the warning system is supposed to provide. Thus, strategic warning can be issued weeks or even months in advance... *Tactical warning* is much more easily defined, although there is some shading in meaning. Strictly defined, tactical warning is not a function of intelligence (at least at the national level) but it is an operational concern. It is warning that that would be available to the commander on the front line..."[7]

But now *everywhere* is the front line. Therefore, I suggest that we redefine terms. "Strategic" reflects the need to mobilize and/or reallocate national assets between guns and butter. "Tactical" reflects the response that can be made with the assets currently in hand. "Warning is an intangible, an abstraction, a theory, a deduction, a perception, a belief. It is the product of reasoning or of logic, a hypothesis whose validity can be neither confirmed nor refuted until it is too late."[8]

Warning is a prediction of the future that matches past and current indicators with a model of the future. Therefore, warning depends very heavily on models or mental images of what the world is and how it works. Building models requires analysis. I contend that we must go one level beyond Ms. Grabo's premise to say that warning intelligence is really warning *analysis*. And the main goal of the warning analyst is to build a model of the world—ourselves, our allies, and our adversaries—through giving current intelligence analysts a context in which they may analyze new reports and observations.

When we navigate, we compare our observations against a map to decide the best direction to take. The high-speed "smart" weapons we use are useless without a highly accurate map with which to guide them, and making accurate maps is a slow, laborious process. Similarly, the high-speed intelligence we provide is useless without a highly accurate "map" of the adversary. Current intelligence analysts need an accurate "map," but warning analysts are required to build and maintain it.

---

[7] Grabo, 4.
[8] Grabo, 4.

This need for analysis and building a conceptual "map" reflects the insights of Col John R. Boyd, USAF, whose thoughts on warfighting are changing the way we operate. Col Boyd is most famous for his collected briefings, *A Discourse on Winning and Losing*, in which he presents and develops the "observation-orientation-decision-action cycle."[9]

//

- Idea of fast transients suggests that, in order to win, we should operate at a *faster tempo or rhythm* than our adversaries—or, better yet, get inside the adversary's *Observation-Orientation-Decision-Action time cycle or loop*.
- Why? Such activity will make us appear ambiguous (unpredictable) thereby generate *confusion* and *disorder* among our adversaries—since our adversaries will be unable to generate mental images or pictures that agree with the *menacing* as well as *faster* transient rhythm or patterns they are competing against.[10]

//

Col Boyd recognizes that operations (Decide and Act) are important but also emphasizes the need for intelligence (Observe and Orient). I suggest that Ms.Grabo's "warning analysis" and Col Boyd's "orientation" are merely different ways of addressing the need for strategic warning by building conceptual "maps" or models. Accordingly, I will also draw heavily on Col Boyd's exposition of the Decision Cycle or OODA Cycle in indicating a path ahead.

> ... it has been deemed prudent and desirable to have indications or warning specialists who, hopefully, will not be burdened or distracted by the competing demands placed on current analysts and will be able to focus their attention solely on potential indications and their analysis in depth.
>
> It is imperative to the process that the facts, including potential or possible facts, and other indications be most diligently and meticulously compiled and analyzed. It is impossible to overemphasize the importance of exhaustive research for warning. It is in the history of every great warning crisis that the post-mortems have turned up numerous relevant facts

[9]Col John R. Boyd, *A Discourse on Winning and Losing,* Collection of un-numbered briefing slides, August 1987. Cited hereafter as Col Boyd.

[10] Col Boyd. Boyd used briefing slides in which what was presented (or left out) and the position of the text on the slide is as important as the text content. Therefore, whenever a whole slide of Col Boyd's is used, it will be indicated by "// Slide //."

> or pieces of information which were available but which, for one reason or another, were not considered in making assessments at the time.[11]

A current intelligence analyst is a news reporter. A warning analyst is much more like a historian or scientist. When a reporter finds a story on a complex or highly technical issue, he or she finds a historian or scientist to provide context. The intelligence community needs dedicated warning analysts to provide that context.

> How can the great machinery of U.S. intelligence, which is capable of spectacular collection and analysis on many subjects, fail to carry out the necessary research in a warning situation? ...there are two obvious difficulties which arise and which may impede the research effort and the surfacing of the relevant facts...
>
> The intelligence research system is set up primarily to analyze certain types of information known as intelligence "disciplines" and on which there is a more or less continuing flow of material... In a crisis situation, great volumes of new material may suddenly be poured into the system. In order to cope, agencies often set up special task forces, and analysts work overtime in an attempt to cover every aspect of the problem...

When it is most needed, communication may break down for sheer lack of time.

> Even more insidious may be the less obvious impending crisis, where the interrelationship of developments is not readily apparent, and particularly where two or more geographic areas may be involved. In such cases, the difficulties of conducting research are greatly compounded when items from two different areas, particularly if they seem relatively obscure or questionable at the time, may not be brought together at all.
>
> The greatest single justification for the existence of separate indications offices or the employment of warning analysts is that they are devoting their full time to research in depth without the distraction of having to fulfill a number of other duties. The warning analyst should never lose sight of the fact that this is his raison d'etre. It is difficult enough to come to a sound warning judgment when all the facts have been considered; it may be impossible without it.[12]

---

[11] Grabo, 7, 9.
[12] Grabo, 10-11, 12.

Warning intelligence requires not only continual, detailed analysis of the adversary but also detailed knowledge of how the adversary interacts with other nations—both allies and adversaries. In short, the warning analyst's first responsibility is Orientation. Such detailed knowledge does not come from pouring money or assets on a single problem then moving on to another but rather by continual attention to interactions and trends—even when there is no crisis. The Intelligence Community will always be in a "crisis management" mode if it only pays attention to problems after they have become crises.

> A time-honored military precept, still quoted with some frequency, holds that intelligence should not estimate the intentions of the adversary, but only his capabilities. Sometimes this has been extended to mean that we can judge his capabilities but that we *cannot* judge his intentions.[13]

In the world of WMD and terrorism, analyzing capabilities but not intentions is not an option. In WMD the only difference between a non-threat dual-use facility and a threatening dual-use facility is intent. In some cases the only difference between a vaccine plant and a BW-agent production plant is that a vaccine plant uses a vaccine strain microorganism and packages it in tiny vials while a BW production plant uses a virulent strain of the same microorganism and packages it in large warheads. Uranium enrichment plants can provide slightly enriched uranium required to fuel a reactor or highly enriched uranium to build a bomb. Chemical plants can provide deadly insecticides to kill insects or deadly chemicals to kill humans. And terrorist groups can potentially exploit benign biological, chemical, or nuclear facilities to obtain deadly materials for WMD. In the age of WMD and terrorism, we *must* "judge his intentions... Unlike current intelligence files, good warning files improve with age."[14]

The more history we know, the more future we can project. The more we know and understand how an adversary acted in the past in response to many different problems, the better we are able to "Orient" so that we can judge his current intentions and his future actions. Not only must we be able to train and retain warning analysts for the long haul, but we also must be able to leverage all the historical data in the many different IC databases to capture not only the indicators they contain but also the models and judgments the warning analysts have made based on that data. "The ability to perceive connections, or at least possible connections, between events and reports which on the surface may not seem to be related is a very important ingredient in the warning process, and one which has

[13] Grabo, 17.
[14] Grabo, 32.

probably been given too little attention."[15] After 9/11 it has become common wisdom that we need to "connect the dots." Ms. Grabo made that clear thirty years ago.

However, in the world of WMD and terrorism, we need to do better. Building models that merely connect the dots tells us what the connections are *now*. In the real world, the connections are not lines but rather vectors—arrows that point to the future.

> If we want to assess an adversary's capabilities, we can do so by "connecting the dots." If we want to assess an adversary's intentions, we need to "orient the arrows."

Therefore, I suggest that we need to reflect on Cynthia Grabo's cogent arguments on the need for warning intelligence and realize that her arguments have become more critical as the world moved out of the Cold War into the Information Age. We also need to reflect on Col Boyd's OODA Cycle and understand that the input required for rational decisionmaking—the Orientation Step—is the responsibility of the warning analyst. We need to find new ways to empower the warning analyst to be able to both "connect the dots" and "orient the arrows" to provide a well-thought-out worldview on which the current intelligence analyst can base his or her assessments. BUT, those warning analyses have to be ready *before* the crisis... For if nations or terrorists use WMD to start the crisis, by then it is already too late.

Rarely does the policymaker or the congressional committee complain that intelligence failed to make an adequate assessment of enemy capabilities, even when this in fact may have been the case. The criticism almost invariably is: "You did not tell me this was going to happen. We were not led to expect this and were surprised." Or, "You mean for all the millions that were spent on collection, you were not able to tell us that this was likely to occur? ...the Intelligence Community's competence often will be judged in the end by the accuracy of its forecasts of what is likely to happen. And indeed this is what the warning business is all about."[16]

---

[15] Grabo, 38.
[16] Grabo, 18.

PROPOSITION

New methodologies for warning intelligence can be developed based on quantum thinking rather than Newtonian thinking.

Chapter 3

FROM NEWTONIAN THINKING TO QUANTUM THINKING

Revolutions in Military Affairs (RMAs) are precipitated by new developments in technology that ultimately change not only strategies and operations but organizations as well. Our current strategies and organizations are based on Industrial-age technologies built by Newtonian thinking. Strategies and organizations for the Information-Age must be built on quantum thinking.

The object of science—just like the object of intelligence—is to predict the future.

Newton's discovery of physical laws and development of calculus as a mathematical system to describe physical systems led to the technological revolution that defined the Industrial Age. Our ability to build engineering marvels, be they automobiles, nuclear weapons, or intercontinental ballistic missiles, is based on our ability to model physical systems quantitatively to predict what they will do when we start them up and send them on their way.

The Newtonian revolution in the physical sciences has led to RMAs based on the new engineering prowess that became possible through our knowledge of physics and chemistry. An Agricultural-Age army equipped with hand-built muskets that could shoot accurately for fifty yards could line up in formation just outside that effective musket range then fix bayonets, charge over fixed positions, and decimate an immobile opponent before that opponent could reload and kill or wound enough attackers to repel the charge. An Industrial-Age army was equipped with mass-produced rifled muskets that could shoot accurately for several hundred yards, and this new technology revolutionized land warfare. As Robert E. Lee found out by ordering Pickett's Charge at Gettysburg, an attacking army faced with the massive longer range firepower of an entrenched Industrial-Age opponent would be decimated long before it even reached the fixed position. Ulysses Grant revolutionized land warfare in the Peninsula Campaign by understanding that a larger better-armed force could prevail by throwing assets into the breach so that in the meat grinder of trench warfare the army that could bring the most weapons to bear for the longest time would prevail.

This paradigm in land warfare prevailed through World War I and was broken by the Nazi blitzkrieg that integrated tanks, aircraft, and better communications into a new paradigm of maneuver warfare. In those revolutions and in that aspect of the current RMA driven by the development of missiles, WMD, and smart bombs, changes in technology that have allowed an army to shoot faster, further, or more accurately have dominated the physical battlefield.

Industrial-Age RMAs were based on Newtonian thinking and the ability to harness the physical world by being able to model physical systems that had predictable characteristics. Industrial-Age intelligence developed along similar lines. Since an opponent's ability to defeat an army depended mainly on the numbers and types of weapons the opponent could build and field, the most important information an Industrial-age analyst could provide was the numbers, types, and locations of the opponent's weaponry. Industrial-Age intelligence analysts were more concerned with an adversary's capabilities than with his intent.

Industrial-Age battlefield dominance was based on physical dominance—both in the ability to field more and better technology than the opponent and in the ability to know where his technology was.

The Newtonian paradigm in science began to unravel at the beginning of the twentieth century with the discovery that energy is discrete or quantal—not continuous. Over the next century several areas of science went through revolutions that occurred almost independently of Newtonian physics:

- Revolutions in quantum physics led to the building of nuclear reactors and nuclear weapons.
- Revolutions in organic chemistry led to the plastics and pharmaceutical industries and the building of chemical weapons.
- Revolutions in biology led to genetic engineering and the building of new kinds of biological weapons.
- Revolutions in silicon chemistry led to the microchip and the computer revolution.

While knowledge of Newtonian physics was critical to all the engineering revolutions of the Industrial Age, not one of these new revolutions was precipitated by Newtonian physics or Newtonian modeling methods based on calculus. This is because all are based on quantum concepts—the fact that the world is built of discrete countable objects such as atoms, molecules, organisms, or electrons—rather than being continuous as Newton assumed when he invented calculus.

I suggest that quantum science will change society in the Information Age just as Newtonian science changed society in the Industrial Age. Every paradigm shift in warfare has gone through three stages: (1) a Military Technical Revolution (MTR) where new technologies give advantage over old ones; (2) a Revolution in Military Affairs (RMA) where new strategies and operational concepts fully exploit the new technology; and (3) a Revolution in Military Culture (RMC) where the operational concepts and technologies are integrated into new kinds of organizations. The MTR precipitated by the mass-produced rifled repeating musket led to the RMA of trench warfare which led to an RMC in which the military totally reorganized to fight that way.

A journey of a thousand miles begins with a single step.
Chinese Proverb

We are at the threshold of a paradigm shift for the Information Age precipitated by quantum thinking that is potentially even larger than the paradigm shift for the Industrial Age precipitated by Newtonian thinking. One cannot know which way to take the first step on a thousand-mile journey unless one knows where that thousand-mile-distant goal is. Similarly, we cannot really define how we should change our strategies, operational concepts, and organizations to best exploit Information-Age technology unless we can see beyond the paradigm shift to what the world might look like in the next two generations. That depends on: (1) understanding what a paradigm shift is and how a culture gets beyond it, and (2) understanding the fundamental differences between Newtonian thinking and quantum thinking that make Newtonian physics and calculus virtually irrelevant in quantum physics, organic chemistry, biology, and computer science—and, therefore, virtually irrelevant in the analysis of the nuclear, chemical, and biological weapons and computers produced by the new paradigm.

Chapter 4

PARADIGM SHIFTS — WHEN THE FUTURE AIN'T WHAT IT USED TO BE

In a paradigm shift, one asks the same question and gets a different answer. The difference depends on the underlying assumptions one makes about the world. Therefore, we must re-examine the assumptions of any paradigm to know when it can be used accurately.

The future ain't what it used to be.
Yogi Berra

One perceptive historian, viewing a classical case of a science's reorientation by paradigm shift, recently described it as "picking up the other end of the stick," a process that involves "handling the same bundle of data as before, but placing them in a new set of relations with one another by giving them a different framework." Others who have noted this aspect of scientific advance have emphasized its similarity to a change in visual gestalt: the marks on paper that were first seen as a bird are now seen as an antelope, or vice versa. That parallel can be misleading. Scientists do not see something else: instead they simply see it.[17]

Thomas Kuhn, *The Structure of Scientific Revolutions*

In a true paradigm shift the world is turned on its head. A proponent of the new paradigm asks the same question as a proponent of the old paradigm, but gets a different answer. An argument then ensues between the dueling paradigms—with no resolution because ultimately paradigms rest on belief systems that can never be proved or disproved, only believed or disbelieved.

Therefore, bridging the gap across a paradigm shift requires changing one's beliefs about how the world works—a difficult task at best. This problem was rampant when, in the early twentieth century, quantum physics began to overturn Newtonian physics. Werner Heisenberg suggested that the huge gap between Newtonian thinking and quantum thinking could be spanned using Niels Bohr's principle of complementarity. But Bohr's principle was designed to reconcile Newtonian mechanics with relativity and quantum theories—which most of us find rather strange if not totally incomprehensible. Therefore,

[17]Thomas Kuhn, *The Structure of Scientific Revolutions* (Chicago, IL: University of Chicago Press, 1996), 85. Cited hereafter as Kuhn.

if we are to use the complementarity principle to best effect, we need to use it on more familiar paradigms.

Let me explain what a paradigm shift is and how the complementarity principle can help us understand it by a more familiar example.

Fill in the blank.
The shortest distance between two points is a ____________________ .

Now on the diagram below, draw the path that describes the shortest distance between point N and M.

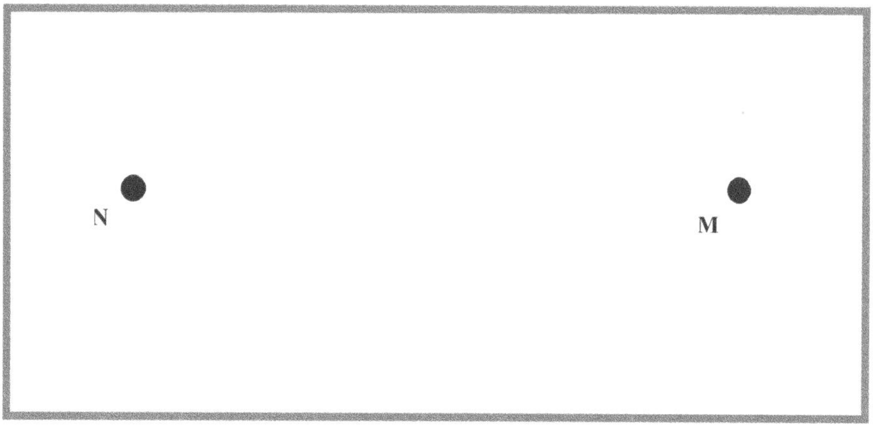

Unless you read ahead, I can virtually guarantee that you filled in the blank with *straight line* and your drawing looked like this.

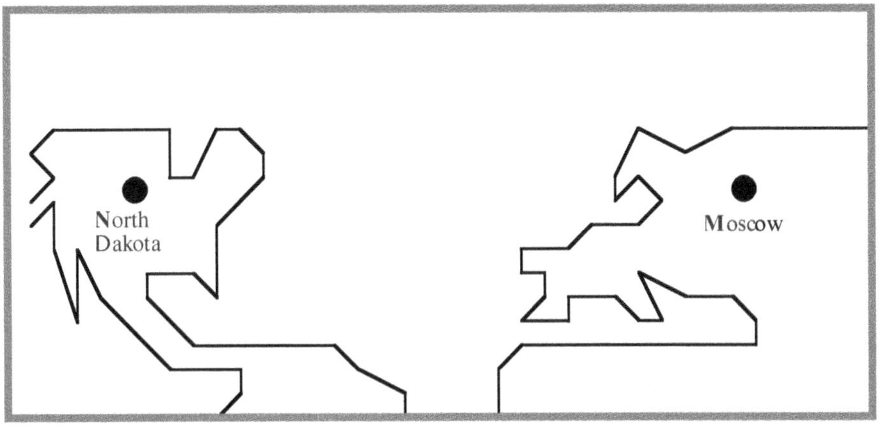

Now on the map below, draw the direction that during the Cold War the Air Force aimed their missiles to take the shortest distance between a silo in North Dakota and a target near Moscow.

Your answer probably looks something like this.

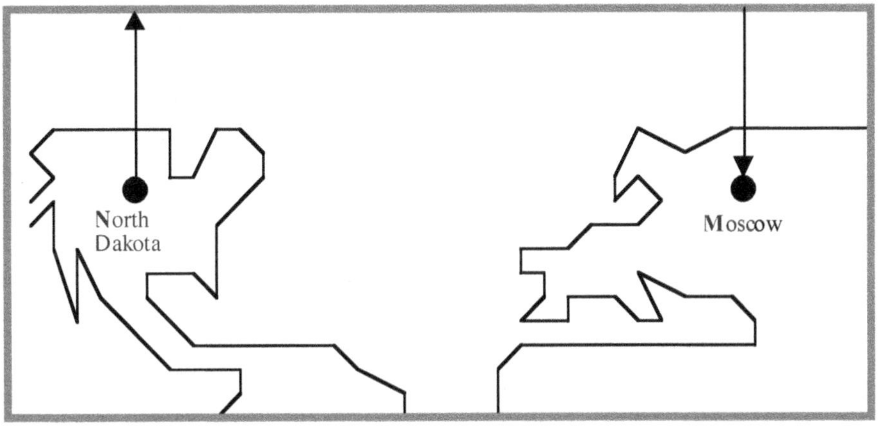

How was it that by merely re-labeling N and M to North Dakota and Moscow that the direction of the path went from directly East to directly North?

Of course the answer is simple. On the earth the shortest distance between two points is a *great circle*—not a *straight line*.

And you're thinking that the first question was a trick question. *How* was it a trick question? We have just been so used to doing geometry on a plane—the Euclidian paradigm—that we virtually never think to do geometry on a sphere—a non-Euclidian paradigm.

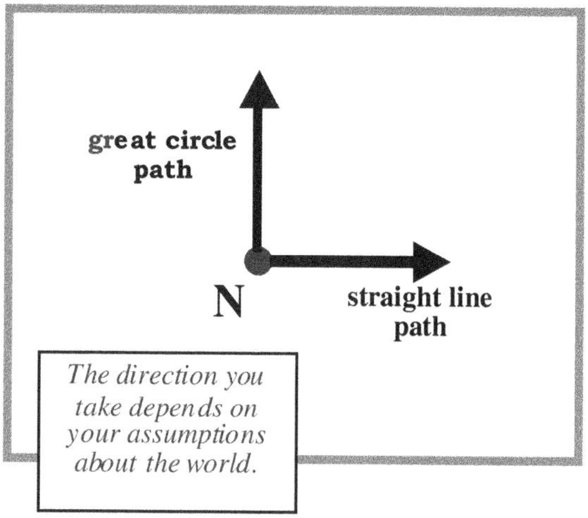

On the other hand, you *can* get to Moscow from North Dakota by going directly east. It is a pathway and it *does* get you there—only it is not the shortest path. So if the earth was as flat as our usual Mercator map depiction of it, the East answer is the correct one.

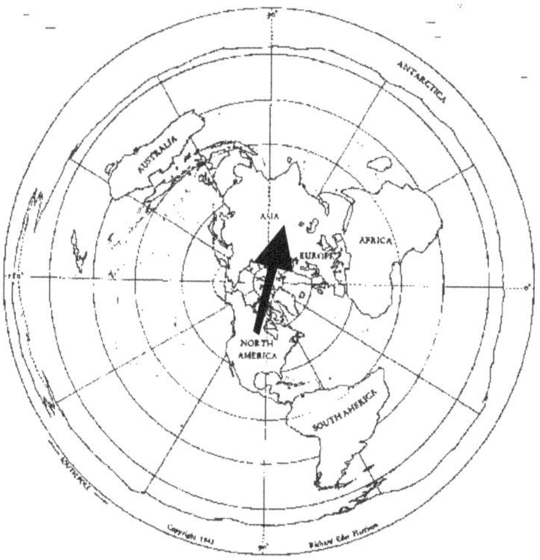

Both the great circle and straight-line paradigms get a correct answer in their own reference frames. So to a proponent of the straight-line paradigm, the North path is wrong. And when the proponent of the great circle paradigm aims his missile north, the straight-line proponent shakes his head and wonders why the other proponent just aimed his missile in the wrong direction.

On the other hand the great-circle proponent sees the most direct route because he sees the world in a different way.

Also, there is no compromise position. Either the East or the North path will, in fact, get to Moscow, but any compromise direction will miss.

Furthermore, if the straight-line proponent offered to compare the paradigms using a much more controlled experiment, such as the direction from Washington to Baltimore or New York to Boston, both paradigms get virtually the same answer. (This is why mariners and pilots use the flat earth Mercator projection for all but the longest sea voyages or intercontinental flights). So, the straight-line proponent is likely to say, "why should I even bother learning your great circle paradigm, when, in the cases that matter, I cannot tell the difference between the two?"

In fact, we use a straight-line flat earth paradigm most of the time anyway, even though we know the earth is round. Have you ever put a globe in the glove compartment of your car?

In paradigm shifts: (1) one asks the same questions but gets different answers; (2) the differences depend on basic fundamental beliefs that cannot be proved or disproved in either paradigm; (3) there are no compromise answers for situations where the assumptions of the two paradigms are at odds; and (4), the two paradigms give the same answers in situations where the assumptions of the old paradigm approximate those of the new.

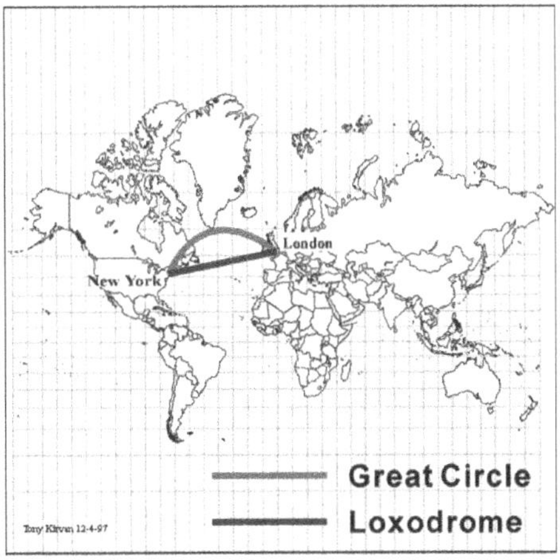

Heisenberg indicated that there can be no grounds for reconciliation between paradigms until both paradigms are developed enough to get to step (4), which is the complementarity principle. More simply stated, the complementarity principle is the idea that models in two different paradigms give the same answer only under conditions where the assumptions of both paradigms are comparable. When one goes from New York to Boston, the shape of the earthly sphere in that small region is almost a plane so that a globe and a flat map are almost indistinguishable. It is only when we know enough about geometry on both planes and spheres to be able to see that plane geometry is a limiting case contained within non-planar geometry that we can be comfortable living with both paradigms. We can look at the chart on the right and believe that the great circle route is actually shorter than the loxodrome (course of constant direction) only because we know that plane geometry (the Mercator projection) works well only for small charts where the surface of the sphere is approximately the same as a plane. Therefore, we are comfortable using maps, and we don't try fitting a globe in our glove compartment and leave great circles for the Air Force, pilots on intercontinental flights, and mariners.

In a paradigm shift, ideas we held dear—sometimes even ideas that we considered "facts"—all of a sudden are either wrong or only work under particular conditions. Consider the following paradigm shifts, and note how we have always asked the same question but sometimes we get a different answer. This does not necessarily totally overturn the old paradigm but limits its applicability. The complementarity principle allows us to see how the limiting old paradigm is contained within and complementary to the new paradigm. It is only by using the complementarity principle that we can comfortably use both the old and the new paradigm.

Old: The earth is *flat*.
New: The earth is *round*.
Complementarity Condition: When the area represented on a chart is small enough to approximate the portion of the sphere as a plane, a map is almost as accurate as a globe.

Old: The *sun* revolves around the *earth*.
New: The *earth* revolves around the *sun*.

Complementarity Condition: When observing the heavens by eye, the epicycles of Ptolemy provide calculations that are almost the same as those using the methods of Copernicus and Keppler.

Old: Atoms are *in*divisible.
New: Atoms are divisible.
Complementarity Condition: See Bohr and Heisenberg...

Therefore, in understanding any paradigm shift, one must go back to the underlying assumptions of both the old and new paradigms to understand how the new paradigm can provide useful answers where the old one is limited by its assumptions. And we can only be comfortable when we can see where they show complementarity. As Kuhn indicated, "The decision to reject one paradigm is always simultaneously the decision to accept another, and the judgment leading to that decision involves the comparison of the paradigms with nature and with each other."[18]

In science our knowledge of the world depends on our ability to model it in terms of a paradigm that supports observations and allows testable experiments from them. In intelligence our knowledge of the world—or our orientation—depends on our ability to understand it in a way that can support observations and reports and allow actionable decisions from them.

---

[18]Kuhn, 77.

In the Industrial Age we based our thinking about intelligence—directly or indirectly because of what we learned in school—on Newtonian scientific methods. If Newtonian science is irrelevant for modeling nuclear physics, organic chemistry, biology, and computer science, then the answers we get by Newtonian methods to questions in those fields will also be irrelevant. More importantly, human organizations and cultures are biological, and if we are going to model them in an actionable way, we need to forget Newton and build a New Science based on quantum principles.

//

ILLUMINATION

- The previous discussion assumes interaction with both the *external* and *internal* environment. Now, let us assume, for whatever reason or combination of circumstances, that we design a command and control system that hinders interaction with the *external* environment. This implies a focus inward, rather than outward.
- Picking up from this idea, we observe from Darwin that:
  - ❑ The environment selects.
  - ❑ Ability or inability to interact and adapt to exigencies of environment select one *in* or *out*.
- Furthermore, according to the Godel Proof, the Heisenberg Uncertainty Principle, and the Second Law of Thermodynamics:
  - ❑ One cannot determine the character or nature of a system within itself.
  - ❑ Moreover, attempts to do so lead to confusion and disorder. Why? Because in the "real world" the environment intrudes (my view).
- Now, by applying the ideas of Darwin, the Second Law, Heisenberg, and Godel to Clausewitz one can see that:

> He who can generate many non-cooperative centers of gravity magnifies friction. Why? Many non-cooperative centers of gravity within a system restrict interaction and adaptability of a system with its surroundings, thereby leading to a focus inward (i.e., within itself), which in turn generates confusion and disorder, which impedes vigorous or directed activity, hence, by definition, magnifies friction or entropy.[19]

//

---

[19]Col Boyd.

Chapter 5

FROM NEWTONIAN ANALOG MODELS TO QUANTUM DIGITAL MODELS

The core assumption of Newtonian calculus is that the world is continuous and single-valued. The real world is, however, demonstrably digital and multi-state. Any kind of model we use to describe the world returns answers that are directly dependent on its underlying core assumptions. An examination of the mismatch of Newtonian models with real-world systems—especially biological systems that include human organizations, cultures, and tools—indicates that several Newtonian assumptions we currently use to analyze those systems' functions provide misleading and/or incomplete assessments. This analysis also points toward the basis of a New Science based on quantum methods, which assume that the world is digital and multi-state.

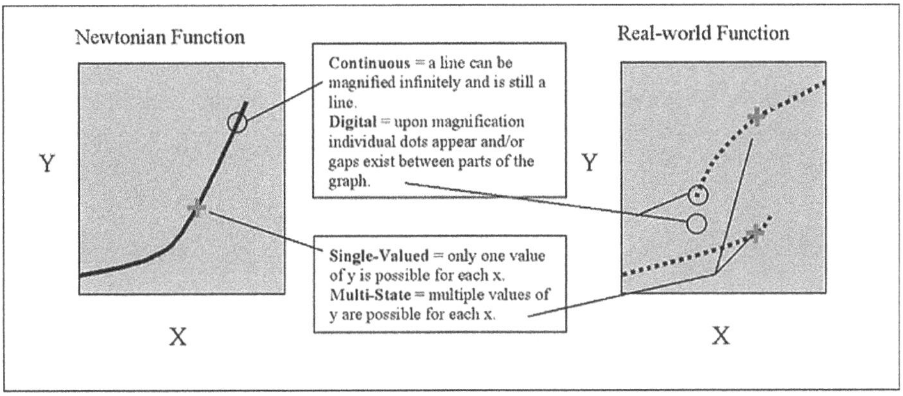

Integral and differential calculus is based totally on the assumptions that mathematical functions can be described by lines that can be subdivided into smaller and smaller pieces *ad infinitum* (that is, continuous or analog) and that there is one and only one value of y for every x (that is, single-valued). In real-world functions when one subdivides the line far enough it becomes a series of unconnected dots (digital) and there can be multiple values of y for each x (multi-state). This seemingly small distinction in our mathematical formalism used to model the world has enormous implications for how our models work and when they become irrelevant. To model the world for the Information-Age we must rely on a New Science that reflects the digital and multi-state nature of the world.

Let me explain by comparing the Newtonian paradigm with the required paradigm for the New Science using conditions in which the two show complementarity. This complementarity is very important here because using the Newtonian paradigm outside these limited complementarity conditions will give incomplete or misleading answers.

Although this is a discussion of the scientific basis by which we model and analyze the world, I will use examples where possible from descriptions of navigation or familiar technologies directly applicable to intelligence analysis. Being able to understand and model navigation is crucial to accommodating the New Science and extending it to a new logical and computational method for intelligence analysis and assessment because: (1) the targets we model—be they weapons of mass destruction or the organizations that build and employ them—need to use navigational methods to function, and (2) we also are navigating when we do such an analysis.

//

ILLUMINATION

- Orientation is the *schwerpunkt.* It shapes the way we interact with the environment—hence orientation shapes the way we *observe*, the way we *decide*, the way we *act.*

In this sense

- Orientation shapes the character of *present* observation-orientation-decision-action loops—while these present loops shape the character of *future* orientation.

IMPLICATION

- We need to create mental images, views, or impressions, hence patterns that match the activity of the world.
- We need to deny our adversary the possibility of uncovering or discerning patterns that match our activity, or other aspects of the reality of the world.[20]

//

[20]Col Boyd.

From Bigger, Faster Technology to Smarter Thinking: History Matters I

Newtonian Assumption: A continuous function describing two point-like objects can predict the future on the basis of a single observation.

New Science Assumption: A digital model of real objects with definable structure can predict the future on the basis of a history of observations in multiple dimensions.

Complementarity Condition: When enough data points have been collected, one can build a model or function that can predict the future with no additional data points.

Example: Given the object observed on the radarscope, predict its future course and speed relative to the object in the center.

Newtonian thinking says that if I have a mathematical function that describes the interaction of two point-like objects, I can use that function to predict their future position and momentum. Unfortunately, if you don't already *have* the function, things can be rather difficult. The Newtonian model works best for the movements of planets, so that the blips on the "radarscope" could represent the earth and moon. In that case the plot would look something like this. If we already know the exact position and momentum (course and speed) of the moon plus the masses of both the earth and the moon we can predict the path of the moon very far into the future.

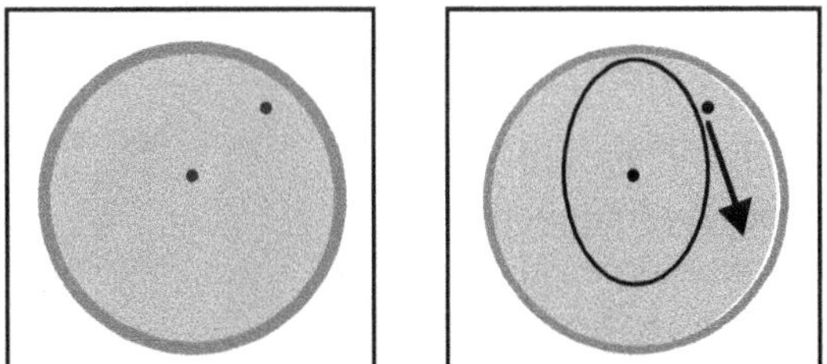

However, if we examine this a bit deeper, we can see that many years worth of observations were required (by Tycho Brahe) of planetary motions before Johannes Kepler could fit them to a curve that described the orbits in terms of Newton's Law's of motion and gravitational interaction. But in real-world situations, the warfighter or intelligence analyst does not have the luxury of collecting all that data and saying, "Now I can predict the future without any more observations merely on the basis of my mathematical functions." What we forget is that the degree of determinism that went into the initial conditions accounts for multiple observations.

Let's return to our real-world radarscope and define all the things we need to observe before we can predict the future motion of our radar blip. On the screen

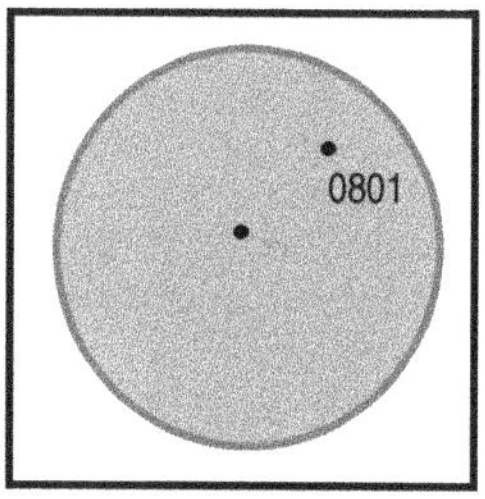

right now we have a position (potentially Lat and Lon) for our own ship in the center and a position for the target (in the form of a bearing and range). We have four data bits on two point-like objects but not enough data to determine a course and speed. Of course, Heisenberg's Uncertainty Principle in quantum physics stated that one cannot determine the position plus the momentum (the scientist's way of saying position plus course and speed) in a single experiment. And every sailor, pilot, or artillery spotter who has ever tried to track a target by radar knows that the real world follows Heisenberg not Newton.

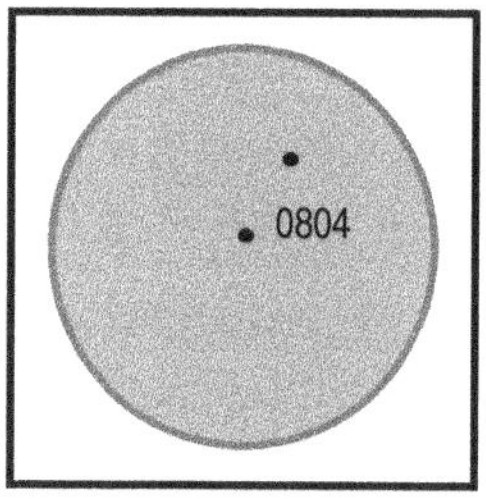

So let's wait a bit and get another look at our radarscope. After three minutes the scope looks like this. What is the course and speed of the target? There's still not enough data by the Newtonian method because we don't have a function to calculate.

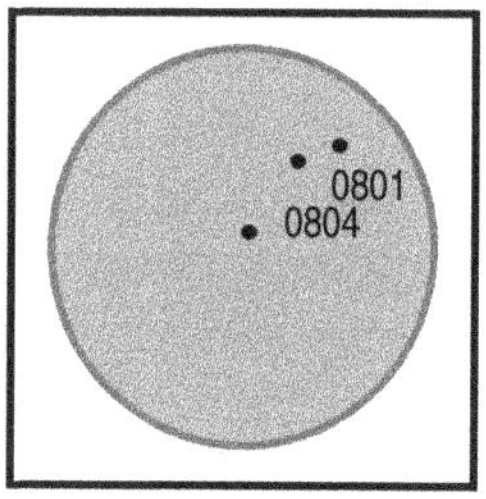

Of course, any sailor, pilot, or artillery spotter can tell that you *do* have enough data to solve for the target's course and speed—but of course you've got to be smart enough to save the historical data. And the savvy operator had already marked the first position on the radarscope with a grease pencil so his scope looks like this. The two points define two positions and simple math will tell us that velocity = [(position 2)-(position 1)] / [(time 2)-(time 1)] or v = Δ (position)/Δ (time).

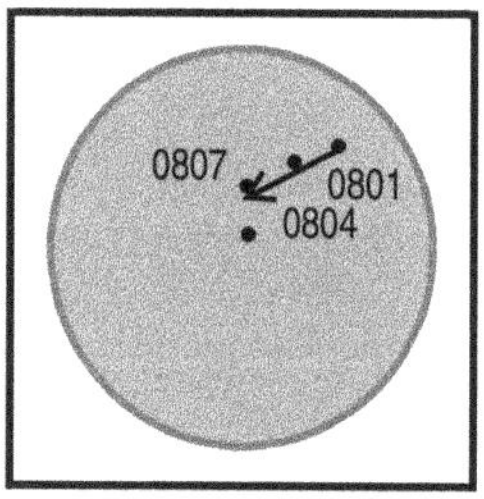

By now another three minutes have passed and there's another blip to add on the scope. By lining up the three dots—one from the present and two historical ones plotted in grease pencil—the operator can read off a course. Then by measuring the distance the blip moved in the six minutes using the range scale of his scope and dividing by the 0.1 hour (= six minutes) he can compute the speed.

But what is the target's position? In the time that it took to do the measurements and calculations, the target moved. But by using the simple function now determined graphically with the grease pencil, the operator can extend the arrow forward and predict where the target will be in three more minutes. And how confident is the operator of his assessment? It depends on how much history he has available.

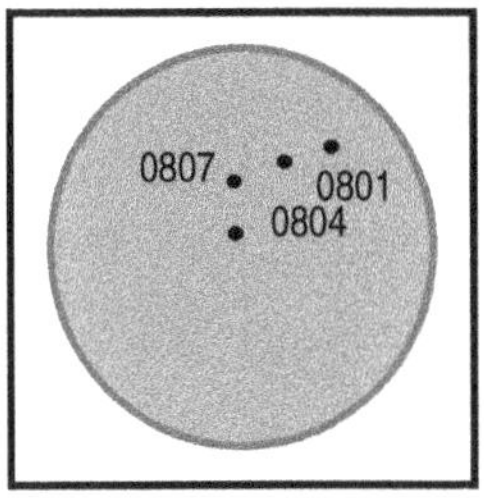

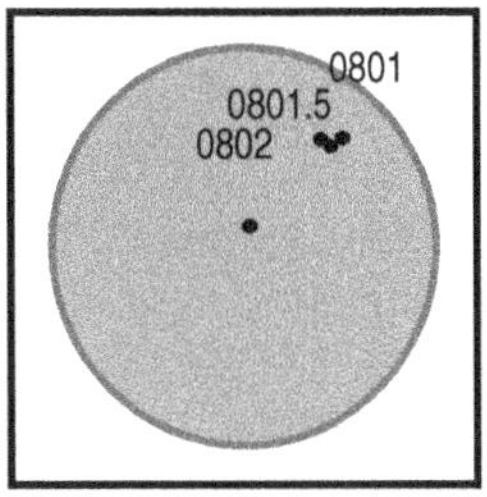

Examine the two plots to the left and decide which one gives you the best estimate of where the target will be three minutes from your last observation. In a real world plot with data scatter, the larger period of history it covers the more accurate the result is—*if* the target has not decided to change course and/or speed.

In Newtonian thinking all functions are equally useful because they can be calculated forward and backward in time with equal accuracy. Note that when you take the entire history, you can get a very accurate estimate of the course and speed but you can only equate that computation in conjunction with an average position that is somewhere spread over the entire track you have measured.

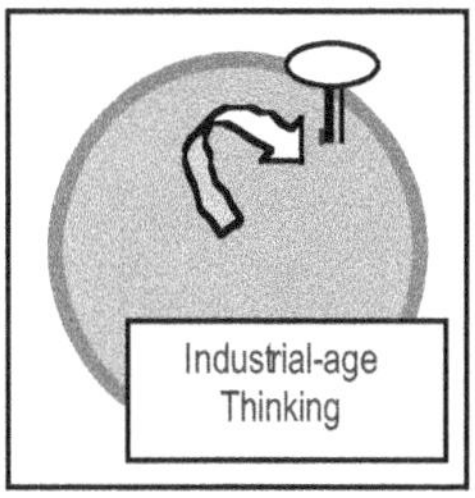

From this simple difference in assumptions, we operate very differently.

Cold War Targeting: The key player on the battlefield is the guy with his finger on the ICBM launch button. The Newtonian Revolution enabled the physical sciences. Technological superiority based on the physical sciences meant weapons that could go farther or faster or carry a bigger boom. Therefore, the missile officer in the North Dakota silo or the B-52 pilot was the key player on the battlefield. History did not matter; solving the course and speed did not matter. If you can deliver nuclear ordnance on target anywhere in the world in fifteen minutes, all you need to know is what the opponent is doing *now*. Imagery Intelligence (IMINT) and Measurement and Signature Intelligence (MASINT) are the keys to Industrial-Age targeting.

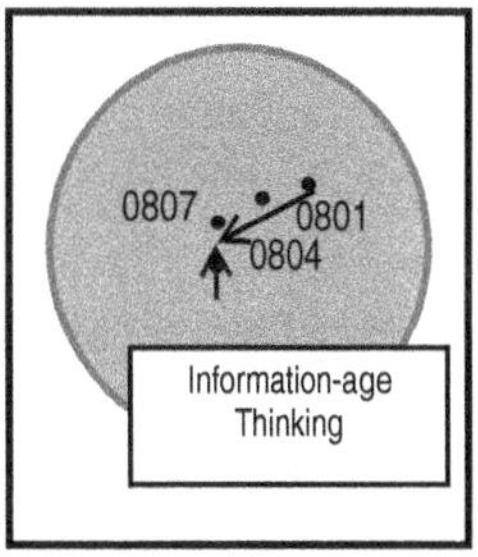

Afghan War Targeting: The key player on the battlefield is the guy on horseback with the binoculars, GPS, and laser-pointer. In the Information Age the more accurately one can determine where the opponent is and what he will do, the more precisely one can target the opponent. Afghanistan showed that a person on the ground is far superior in determining the location of an opponent and tracking his intentions than all the high-tech remote-sensing devices—mainly for his ability to loiter and maintain a history of the opponent—and determining his location and intentions. A smart bomb is only as smart as the spotter or analyst who determines target PIM (position and intended movement). HUMINT is the key to Information-age targeting.

The take-home message here is that the idea of an exact mathematical function that can tell you everything you need to know about the future of even a simple point-like object based on a single observation is a classroom dream based on a Newtonian model of the world. In the real world—History Matters! The quantum reality of the Heisenberg Uncertainty Principle applies and:

- You need a historical record of observations to be able to assess a target's motion. You cannot tell where something is going unless you know where it came from.
- If it moves faster or goes farther, you will be able to assess its course and speed more accurately but you will be able to assess its position less accurately (just as Heisenberg said).

In the Industrial Age, IMINT and MASINT were critical for targeting, and analysis did not really matter—only how fast you can turn your observation of what is happening now into action. In the Information-Age HUMINT plus selected Industrial-Age legacy weapons, will be critical for targeting, and analysis of the historical record is crucial to understand the opponent's intentions and future actions.

//

SAMPLES FROM HISTORICAL ENVIRONMENT

- **Sun Tzu (around 400 BC)**
  Probe enemy to unmask his strengths, weaknesses, patterns or movement and intentions. Shape enemy's perception of world to manipulate/undermine his plans and actions. Employ Cheng/Ch'I maneuvers to quickly and unexpectedly hurl strength against weakness.
- **Napoleon (early 1800s)**
  "Strategy is the art of making use of time and space. I am less chary of the latter than the former. Space we can recover, time never. ...I may lose a battle, but I shall never lose a minute. The whole art of war consists in a well reasoned and circumspect defensive, followed by an audacious attack."
- **N.B. Forrest (1860s)**
  "Git thar the fustest with the mostest."
- **Blumetritt (1947)**
  "The entire operational and tactical leadership method hinged upon...*rapid* concise assessment of situations,...*quick* decisions and *quick* execution, on the principle: 'each minute ahead of the enemy is an advantage.'"
- **Balck (1980)**
  Emphasis on creation of *implicit connections or bonds* based upon *trust, not*

mistrust, yet that permit wide freedom for subordinates to exercise imagination and initiative—yet, harmonize within intent of superior commanders. Benefit: internal simplicity that permits rapid adaptability.

- **Yours Truly**
  Operate inside the adversary's observation-orientation-decision-action loops to enmesh adversary in a world of uncertainty, doubt, mistrust, confusion, disorder, fear, panic chaos, ...and/or fold adversary back inside himself so that he cannot cope with events/efforts as they unfold.[21]

//

Thinking in *time* is as important as thinking in *space*. Col Boyd make this message very clear on three levels: (1) history matters—we can learn from the strategic thinking of analysts all the way back to Sun Tzu; (2) the best military thinkers talked processes over objects; and (2) the OODA Cycle exists in time, not space.

From Fighting against Technologies to Out-Thinking Decisionmakers: History Matters II

Newtonian Assumption: The world is single-valued.

New Science Assumption: The world is multi-state.

Complementarity Condition: Where the system being modeled is very far from a decision (bifurcation) point, one can use the Newtonian single-valued model.

Example: An air conditioner thermostat is set at 70 degrees. For stable control and to ensure it is not constantly cycling ON and OFF, the thermostat will turn the air conditioner ON when the temperature rises to 71 degrees and turn it off when it has cooled the room to 69 degrees. I have two photographs of the thermostat: one that I just took that shows a temperature reading of 70

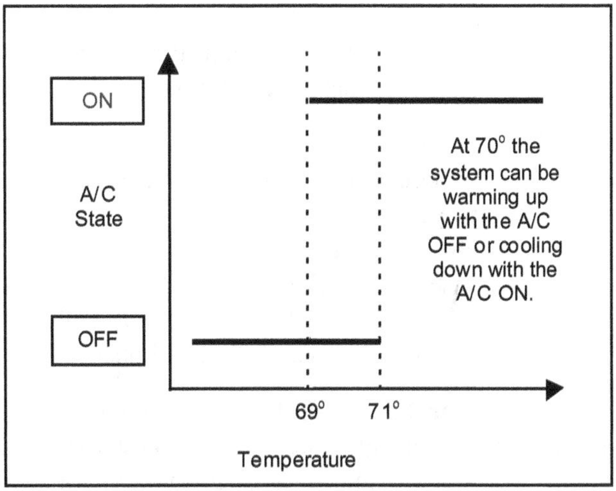

[21]Col Boyd.

degrees and one I took six minutes ago that shows the temperature at 71 degrees. Is the air conditioner ON or OFF?

This is a problem that is totally unsolvable in the Newtonian paradigm which depends on instantaneous information to calculate its functions—and at 70 degrees the air conditioner can be either ON or OFF dependent on its history. The Newtonian paradigm will give a proper answer if the temperature is above 71 degrees (always ON) or below 69 degrees (always OFF) because at those temperatures there is only one solution. However, within the controlling "dead-band" between 69 and 71 degrees, no answer is possible by Newtonian methods because there are two correct answers: the air conditioner is ON if it was above 71 degrees a few minutes ago and it's cooling the room, or the air conditioner is OFF if it was below 69 degrees a few minutes age and the room is warming up for the next cooling cycle. In the New Science the answer is ON because it appears to be on the cooling cycle based on the historical observation. Therefore, to describe a multi-state system—one that is capable of making decisions—Newtonian methods work only when the decision already has been irreversibly made. And even in the New Science, one will require a history of events to determine which of the multiple states the system is in now.

Unfortunately, it's even more complicated than that. The two photos show that the air conditioner is ON because it appears to be on the cooling cycle. However, that assumes that the length of the cooling cycle is more than six minutes; if the cooling cycle is only three minutes the first picture could have been taken right at the beginning of a cooling cycle and the second could have been taken after the air conditioner was OFF and the temperature drifted back up to 70 degrees. To get a correct answer, even in the New Science, one will need enough pictures taken over at least three cycles to be confident in knowing what the cooling cycle length is...which will also will be different if the temperature outdoors is 85 degrees or 110 degrees. History matters even more.

Cold War Targeting: Shoot them all, and you'll get the one you want. With weaponry that could shoot faster and farther and with a bigger boom, the advantage was always with the side that shot first. In the Industrial-Age, pre-emptive strike was always the best answer. Therefore, intelligence was set to be very generic because fast reaction was key, and the old saying goes "nukes mean never having to say you've missed." Therefore, the missile officer did not need to know anything more than, "If I get the order, I push the button, and a city disappears."

Afghan War Targeting: Only shoot the ones who have decided to shoot you. In the Information Age, one needs to know more about an opponent. In Afghanistan it was not a viable strategy to shoot anyone carrying a gun because everyone in Afghanistan carries a gun, or even to shoot at anyone who's shooting because they're not always shooting at you. No simple "If X then Y" Newtonian rules are possible when party goers at a wedding will shoot guns in the air that appear at first glance like Taliban gunfire. One needs to model the decisionmakers to know which state they're in before firing: the "shooting in the air at a wedding" state, or the "shooting at incoming aircraft" state—and that kind of knowledge requires history. In the Information Age, proportional and logical response must be the norm.

Intelligence analysts are expected to predict future events and trends based on observations of the world. Biological systems—be they individual organisms like bacteria or humans or collections of organisms like countries or even the tools constructed by human organisms—make decisions and control their own behavior in response to their environment. In our simple example, we require at least three control cycles worth of data (dependent on today's outdoor temperature) plus two additional photographs to confidently assess whether the air conditioner is ON or OFF. And that is for a single thermostat, which can only turn ON or OFF in response to a single-input temperature sensor.

The take-home message here is that decisionmaking systems—as simple as thermostats or as complex as states building WMD—are multi-state and cannot be calculated in the Newtonian paradigm unless they are far enough away from the particular set of conditions that will trigger the decision. The New Science must, therefore, account for systems that can exist in different states under different conditions. One cannot predict what a system will do unless one knows what it did in the past. And once again—History Matters! The New Science must be able to model the decisionmaking process.

Industrial-Age intelligence was based on Newtonian models that totally ignored decisionmaking. Therefore, there was only one best strategy—preemptive strike—for any adversary because the adversary's decisionmaking process was not even considered in defining policy, and winning was only dependent on our own decisions and actions.

Information-Age intelligence must be based on quantum models that can account for the adversary's decisionmaking process. Since an adversary's "state" depends not only on what he is trying to accomplish but also where he is in that decision loop; the Information-Age analyst must be able to provide different options that depend on the adversary's different "states" as well as an estimate of which "state" he is currently in—and hopefully an estimate of which state we would like to push him into.

//

MESSAGE

- Suppress tendency to build-up *explicit internal* arrangements that *hinder interaction* with the *external* world.

  Instead

- Arrange settings and circumstances so that leaders and subordinates alike are given opportunity to continuously *interact* with *external* world, and each other, in order to *more quickly* make many-sided implicit cross-referencing projections, empathies, correlations, and rejections as well as create the similar images or impressions, hence a similar implicit orientation, needed to form an organic whole.

  Why?

- A *similar implicit orientation* for commanders and subordinates alike will allow them to:

  - Diminish their friction and reduce time, thereby permit them to:
  - Exploit variety/rapidity while maintaining harmony/initiative, thereby permit them to:
  - Get inside the adversary's O-O-D-A loops, thereby:
  - Magnify adversary's friction, and stretch-out his time (for a favorable mismatch in friction and time), thereby:
  - Deny the adversary the opportunity to cope with events/efforts as they unfold.[22]

//

The Newtonian paradigm only deals with the physical world. The New Science must deal with the conceptual world. Even as simple a control system as a thermostat uses an OODA Cycle to Observe the world, Orient against its internal model whether that world is too hot or cold enough, Decide whether the air conditioner should be ON or OFF, and Act to ensure that it is in the proper state. Therefore, we need not only to understand the adversary's OODA Cycle but our own as well before we can provide the proper orientation to make the best decision.

---

[22]Col Boyd.

From Targeting Objects to Targeting Individuals

Newtonian Assumption: The world is continuous.

New Science Assumption: The world is digital.

Complementarity Condition: When the world is viewed at a level of granularity that is too large to detect individuals, the strategy will reflect only an "average" response that neglects differences among individuals.

Example 1: If one thousand honeybees can collect one thousand grams of pollen in one hour, in the same time how many grams can half-a-honeybee collect? In the Newtonian world, the answer is calculated to be half-a-gram; in the biological world the answer is zero grams because half-a-honeybee is dead. Therefore, Newtonian thinking only works under conditions where individuals don't matter.

Example 2: If two percent of the female population is pregnant, and we select twenty-five females from that population, how many of them will be pregnant? In the Newtonian world you will find half a pregnant female; in the biological world all you can say is each individual has a two percent chance of being pregnant, but in each case the answer is either yes or no—one cannot be half-pregnant. Newtonian thinking ignores individuals and can, therefore, only describe an "average" individual or theoretically, one individual in a population where all are identical.

The take-home message here is that in biological—and human—systems, the whole is not just the sum or the average of the parts. Individuals matter! There are properties and behaviors that are characteristic of an individual that cannot be subdivided any further. The New Science must, therefore, be able to account for individuality within populations.

From a Two-Player Zero-Sum-Game to a Multi-Player Non-Zero-Sum Game

Newtonian Assumption: All organizations are identical.

New Science Assumption: All organizations are individuals in their own right with differing characteristics dependent on the individuals that comprise them.

Complementarity Condition: When organizations are so simple that the individuals who comprise them can be ignored (either because they are all identical or because only a single individual speaks for the entire organization), then the organization will have only a single "center of gravity" which defines all its actions and vulnerabilities.

Example: I see a large mammal with a furry coat. Is it a threat? The Newtonian answer is that it's large and anything large must be a threat. The biological-quantum-answer is "It all depends." If it's a lion and I have no gun, it's a threat; if it's a lion, and I have a gun, it's game, but it might be a threat if I drop my gun; if it's an antelope and I have no gun, it's not a threat; if it's an antelope and I have a gun, it's not a threat even if I drop my gun. Newtonian models are two-player zero-sum games; answers are always "yes" or "no" in the Newtonian world. Once I know enough information to determine the most important single factor in making the model, then there's only a "yes" or "no" answer. The quantum or biological model needs to collect enough data to discern characteristics of the organism or organization. This is based on the assumption that there are individual characteristics of an organization since it is built of non-identical individuals, be it an organism built of individual cells or an organization built of individual organisms. A pride of lions is very different from a herd of antelopes or a herd of cattle when estimating whether it is a threat to an individual human or to group of cowboys.

Biological organisms are organizations made of different kinds of individuals and organizational thinking depends on very subtle differences in the makeup of those organisms. This makes biological models multiple player non-zero sum games. Each individual organization will have its own goals for survival and its own definition of winning. Put a lion and a deer together and for the lion a "win" is dinner while for the deer a "win" is survival. Add a hyena and the lion might have two choices for dinner while the hyena is rooting for the lion because its dinner is leftovers; and in any case the antelope just wants to survive.

The New Science must account for differences in organizations and must be able to account for non-zero-sum games. In any biological system, the best answer is the win-win scenario. Newtonian models don't even consider that option.

Cold War Intelligence: It is "Us" versus "Them," and the World is bipolar. In the Cold War the only decisionmakers who mattered were the Politburo; everyone else was just following orders. Since the Cold War was built on the assumption that "Communism" was a monolithic entity, the level of granularity in decision-making needed only to assume Us vs. Them. Therefore, we needed only consider dictators who were on "Our Side" or "Their Side;" by that definition Saddam Hussein was a "Good Guy." We also only needed to consider who was fighting on "Our Side," not why they were; in the Cold War world we could ignore the reasons that Islamic nations might choose to fight Communism because the adage "the enemy of my enemy is my friend" was all the rationale we needed. This method of intelligence analysis also resulted in an emphasis on assessing capability to the exclusion of assessing intent. If we assume that every individual is either "with us" or "against us," we don't need to know their intent to any level of granularity more than that; but we do need to know what their capabilities are so we can assess how large a threat they are if they are "against us." Intelligence in the Newtonian zero-sum game world was easy: (1) pick the biggest threat; (2) divert all your intelligence assets in a huge task force to find its center of gravity; (3) defeat its center of gravity and it will crumble. When you are done, find the next biggest threat and repeat the process.

Afghan War Intelligence: It is a multi-polar world where every country, organization, and individual has distinct goals and decisionmaking processes to reach those goals. Finding allies with common goals could work toward win-win scenarios. Not only were the Taliban, Northern Alliance, and Al Qaeda distinct organizations, but also one could expect both the leaders and individual citizens in each of the organizations to make decisions differently. The U.S. found correctly that the multiple factions within Afghanistan had their own cultures and goals. This meant that by encouraging the Northern Alliance we found our "eyes" on the ground to provide the valuable HUMINT targeting we needed to distinguish between Taliban, Al Qaeda, and just your average citizen, truck, or wedding celebration. However, this also required a realization that the Northern Alliance would then become a player in the new government that would rebuild Afghanistan according to an Afghan "win" scenario. It also meant that once the war was headed toward victory, the Taliban rank-and-file became a political problem rather than a military one; since to the Northern Alliance the Taliban were also fellow Afghans, Taliban rank-and-file were re-assimilated within the Afghan populace while the Taliban leadership disappeared because their power base was gone. On the other hand, Al Qaeda fighters—who were mainly non-Afghans anyway—disappeared to regroup elsewhere and remain a significant threat.

Industrial-Age intelligence ignored both the quantum nature of organizations and the fact that individuals even exist. Therefore, intelligence analysts only needed to estimate if they were on "Our Side" or "Their Side"—being an "enemy of my enemy" was a sufficient estimate for decisionmaking. It also led to a simplistic model of the world where a "center of gravity" was all that one needed to find to solve the intelligence problem once and for all.

Information-Age intelligence analysis must account for individuality—both at the organizational level and the individual level. The Information-Age intelligence analyst must be knowledgeable of not only the overall organization but its infrastructure, its leadership, and its culture as well. The Information-Age analyst must assess intent at least as well as he or she assesses capability.

In WMD analysis, these distinctions are critical. Clearly any nation that possesses WMD is a potential threat. Certainly, the most important questions a U.S. policymaker needs to know about a country that possesses WMD are, "Is it a threat? What should I do about that threat? How do I respond when that state's leader goes against U.S. interests?"

In the Newtonian bi-polar world the answers were easy because in the Newtonian world "one size fits all" and every organization is the same. Intelligence was done by assessing capabilities and WMD capability, which, once assessed, ended the intelligence problem with no further analysis. "Yes, any nation that possesses WMD is a threat. We should preemptively end that threat by causing that state to disarm or cause a regime change to make that happen. Who the other country's leader is does not even matter; WMD is a threat and must be ended and any leader who thinks his country should possess WMD should be 'taken out' and a new regime put in place."

In the Information-Age world the answer is "it all depends." Just as all "large mammals" are different, all "nations possessing WMD" are different and have different kinds of leadership and different national goals. Where do we draw the line on "regime change" as the only way to end the WMD problem—with Saddam Hussein and Iraq? Kim Chong-Il and North Korea? Ayatollah Khatami and Iran? President Musharraf and Pakistan? Vladimir Putin and Russia? Ariel Sharon and Israel? Jaques Chirac and France? Tony Blair and Great Britain?

Surely WMD proliferation is the most important intelligence problem of the twenty-first century. But analysts cannot hope to provide policymakers any options other than "find all their WMD facilities and take them out preemptively" until the IC has analytical tools that account for individuality—in countries, the organizations, and cultures that they are built on, and the personalities that lead them.

Information-Age intelligence must be able to assess both capability and intent. Intelligence analysts need new methodologies and tools that can transcend Newtonian Industrial-Age thinking to be able to provide cogent assessments and provide policymakers options that are individual-specific; not "one size fits all." Saddam Hussein, Kim Chong-Il, Perez Musharraf, Ariel Sharon, Jaques Chirac, and Tony Blair can all employ WMD should it come to be in their national interests to do so—which is only in the U.S. national interest when their national interests coincide with that of the U.S. Clearly, there are differing options to deal with these individual leaders and their individual nations. The New Science of Intelligence for the Information Age needs to be able to define those options clearly and distinctly.

Therefore, we need to rethink our intelligence methodologies and tools built for the Industrial Age using Newtonian thinking and replace them with ones built for the Information Age built using quantum thinking. The core of Industrial-Age intelligence was assessment of capabilities. The core of Information-Age intelligence must be assessment of intent.

//

MESSAGE

Referring back to our previous discussion, we can say: orientation *is an interactive process* of *many-sided implicit cross-referencing projections, empathies, correlations, and rejections* that is *shaped by* and *shapes* the interplay of *genetic heritage, cultural tradition, previous experiences*, and *unfolding circumstances*.[23]

//

Assessment of capabilities was built on understanding and identifying things—weapons and the facilities that make them. Assessment of intent must be built on understanding people *as individuals* and the organizations, countries, and cultures they build—for it is people who build WMD.

---

[23] Col Boyd.

Chapter 6

TOWARD NOVEL INTELLIGENCE FROM MASSIVE DATA

Data can be "massive" both in quantity and type. A major problem in exploiting the massive quantities of data available to the Intelligence Community is the lack of a historical baseline and a lack of librarians and curators to organize and tag the data for easy retrieval. This means that we must develop methods for rapid writing of classified history and for systematic data archiving. Data can also be "massive" in its dimensionality. Collecting and analyzing massive amounts of data will not provide valid assessments unless the dimensionality of the data reflects the dimensionality of the problem.

We must reconcile ourselves to the fact that the Community is unlikely to hire human librarians and curators to support analysts in the way that other information-dependent organizations support their researchers. This means that we must develop methods to bypass the need for librarians and curators by automating those functions, that is, developing computer tools for data archiving and retrieval.

Data can also be "massive" in their dimensionality. Collecting and analyzing massive amounts of data will not provide valid assessments if the dimensionality of the data does not reflect the dimensionality of the problem. Moreover, analytical methods are required to assess both current position and projected intentions. Methodologies that hope to project target intentions into the future must be based on data collection for a longer time period into the past; current intelligence data cannot be used to build warning intelligence.

The analyst is swamped with data on a day-to-day basis. There is so much information out there that too little time exists to be able to use it to answer the questions that need to be answered. We need to find ways to be able to wade through the massive amount of data "out there" and use it to find the "nuggets" we need to answer those questions. A current project funded by the Advanced Research Development Activity to address that issue is call NIMD, or "Novel Intelligence from Massive Data."

The NIMD charter suggests that "massive" data are those that are either too large in quantity or in too heterogeneous a format for us to be able to use effectively. I suggest that this well-intentioned answer and the methodology used to pursue it is in fact a straight line, flat-earth approach using Newtonian Industrial-Age thinking, whereas we need a great circle spherical-earth approach using Digital-Information thinking. Newtonian thinking is a paper-and-pencil approach that is inherently a 2-D method to model continuous single-valued systems, so any methodology we build using a Newtonian model must also be inherently 2-D, continuous, and single-valued. Therefore, before we can truly find "novel" intelligence from "massive" data, we must re-define what we mean by "novel" and "massive" for an Information-Age model that is N-dimensional, digital, and multistate.

What is "Novel" Intelligence?

"Novel" is defined as "new and unusual, especially being the first of its kind." Current efforts such as NIMD concentrate on the first part of the definition, "new and unusual." However, as I will shortly show, finding "new and unusual" intelligence data in enormous quantities is *not* a problem—so long as it is not the first of its kind. The challenge for the Information Age is to be able to find intelligence that is "the first of its kind" within an enormous dataset where the required data has not been structured by conventional techniques.

The Industrial-Age definition of "novel" is—new and unusual within the current model but not the first of its kind.

The Information-Age definition of "novel" must be—new and unusual and the first of a totally new kind of data requiring a new model to understand.

What is "Massive" Data?

The Industrial-Age definition of "massive" data is—data whose sheer, enormous quantity is too great for our methodologies to exploit.

I suggest that the Information-Age definition of "massive" data must be—data whose dimensionality is too great for our methodologies to exploit. I can indicate this by two examples:

- A simple research project that shows that sheer quantity of data is *not* an issue for even a neophyte trained in Information-Age methodologies as long as the data are of a kind that has already been modeled.
- A simple data-reduction problem that shows that dimensionality of data can require a total rethink of how we exploit that data even when the dataset contains only four data points and four observations associated with those data points.

Example 1 — An 8th Grade Science Project In the Information Age

Just recently my younger daughter, who is an 8th grader, came home with a science project to find out about an "American inventor who invented something that is smaller than 6 inches" and no further instructions. On first glance one would think that her problem is equivalent to the intelligence analyst's project to find out about an "Iraqi scientist capable of inventing a new BW agent." But it cannot be because she could finish her inventor project in about six hours with a tiny amount of parental guidance and no research budget while the IC is spending millions of dollars and employing teams of highly trained analysts and collectors on the Iraqi scientist problem. Besides, the IC team has access to many times the data in many relational databases but my daughter has only her Internet browser and a library card. Surely my daughter has a NIMD problem because the amount of data she needs to sort through on the Internet and library is truly "massive" in the Industrial-Age definition of "very large." Why is her problem so much easier than that of the Iraqi WMD analysts?

I suggest that there are four major differences in the American inventor problem and the Iraqi scientist problem that make my daughter's project a single Sunday afternoon's work and the Iraqi WMD analyst's a daunting challenge. And note that none of these differences have anything to do with the sheer size or heterogeneity of the respective datasets:

(1) Historians have already collected, parsed, and modeled inventors and inventions using very old, tried and true research techniques but the IC has yet to do the in-depth historical research required for the scientist and BW agent problem.

(2) The librarians have already cataloged all the current material on inventors and inventions using very old, tried and true library science techniques, but the IC has yet to build the kind of library required for the scientist and BW agent problem.

(3) My daughter can easily search the enormous quantity of data on the Internet using the Google search engine because she already had a model for her inventor but the IC is hampered by its lack of a specific model for their scientist.

(4) Although my daughter's project is "novel" for her because it is "new and unusual" it is not truly "novel" because it is not the "first of its kind" in that many other people and students have asked the same question. The Iraqi WMD analyst's project is "novel" in both senses of the word because no one has ever considered how Iraq's BW program has grown historically—certainly not at the classified level.

Faced with the task of finding the "American inventor who invented something smaller than six inches" my daughter asked me to take her to the library and said, "Dad, please help me. I don't even know where to start." So I went to the online catalog, searched for "inventor" and "invention" and by scanning the myriad titles noticed that virtually all were tied to Library of Congress (LC) Call Number "609." I told her we would look for the books with "609," we then read the LC numbers on the shelves until we found them, and I started handing her books with that number that had to do with inventors and inventions...and she did the rest...all in an afternoon's work.

What call number does the Iraqi analyst need to retrieve the data on Iraqi biologists and microbiologists? Or even more fundamentally—if there is a call number for Iraqi biologists, are there any books on the topic? And once we have the names of the inventor or scientist, how do we learn more?

In today's world that is easy for finding American inventors but impossible for finding Iraqi BW scientists for several reasons:

New Knowledge is Built on a Baseline of Old Knowledge Built by Historians

The IC dataset is "massive" because there are no historians to provide perspective on what it means.

There are no *classified* historical baselines because there are no historians in the IC. Most of the intelligence data are currently in the form of text messages residing in multiple databases. The Iraqi analysts could get off to a good start on their project by finding classified books such as "The History of Iraqi Science," or "A Decade of Evading the UN Weapons Inspectors." But such books do not exist. Historians can provide an excellent baseline on many issues of interest to the intelligence analyst, but only from unclassified records. They don't have access to the billions of text messages in IC databases, but the IC does not employ any of its own historians to build such a baseline. And analysts do not have the time—or don't stay on one project long enough—to build the historical baseline that gives context for their current analysis. My daughter can rapidly find information on American inventors and their inventions because there are historians writing books about them; the Iraqi analysts cannot do the same because there are no historians writing classified books on WMD programs anywhere.

IC Challenge: How can we build the historical baseline with no historians? How can we automate the function of those absent classified historians with smart computer programs?

Information Retrieval is Built on Library Science by Librarians

The IC classified datasets are virtually impossible to use because there are no librarians to catalog and meta-tag them.

There is no catalog of classified documents because is no National Library of the IC. One can very rapidly find books on any imaginable topic in a library catalog because a librarian somewhere took the time to assign a Library of Congress number. Think of how hard it would be to use a library if there were no librarians—only computer engineers to maintain the computers—and all the books were placed randomly on the shelves without anyone assigning Library of Congress codes. My daughter could easily retrieve the half-dozen books on American inventors and then use the Tables of Contents and Indices to choose one who invented something "smaller than six inches"—having quickly found the inventors of the paper clip, the computer mouse, and many others. The intelligence analysts have no such ability to do the same because in the IC, libraries only have unclassified source materials, and classified documents are stored online in databases compiled by computer engineers without librarians to oversee the cataloging and indexing that the rest of the world uses to make data retrieval easy.

IC Challenge: How do we catalog and index the IC products both hard copy and online on Intelink for easy retrieval of relevant documents? How do we replace the missing librarians by smart computer programs?

There is no meta-tagging for easy document retrieval because there are no librarians to maintain IC databases. One can also find records very rapidly in a huge database like the National Institutes of Health's online PubMed database of biological research because the National Library of Medicine (NLM) hires librarians to meta-tag every journal article in a standard format for authors, titles, affiliations and to select a list of keywords on that article on the basis of a standard NLM ontogeny. PubMed is easy to use because *every* scientific paper that is abstracted in that database is read individually and meta-tagged by a real person at the NLM, usually called a curator. The IC has hired many different IT contractors to develop ontologies for IC records—reinventing the Library of Congress codes and specialized ontologies of the NLM and other specialized databases. Ontologies do not work until they are assigned to each individual record—and there are no curators in the IC who do so.

IC Challenge: How can we meta-tag existing documents in IC databases and provide policies for easily meta-tagging new ones? How do we replace all the missing data curators with smart computer programs?

There is No Easy Way to Data-mine Heterogeneous Data Sets Because Historical Baselines are not Available for IC Analysts

Once my daughter found an "invention less than six inches" and the name of the inventor from the general studies in the library books, finding additional data on the Internet was very simple using the Google search engine and looking for records that contain that inventor's name and/or the name of the invention. In any data-mining search of heterogeneous data on the Internet, the key is finding a specific starting point such as a person's name plus an associated fact (such as their invention or where they work or what their expertise is). Potentially, the Iraqi analysts could search for all the "anthrax" experts who work at universities in "Baghdad," but there are so many possible pairs of keywords that could apply to "an Iraqi scientist capable of producing a BW agent" that pairing them one by one is prohibitive. One needs the clues from the more generic search of the historical baseline.

IC Challenge: How can we provide data-mining profiles for data retrieval that can work independently of a historical baseline? Again, how do we replace the missing historians with smart computer programs?

Discovery of "Novel" Intelligence Requires Re-searching the Data Using New Models

Data-mining is easy for tracking known entities with known interactions, but virtually impossible for identifying new kinds of interactions with unknown entities—even if the data are contained in the dataset.

My daughter's project was not "novel" because ultimately she was merely retrieving and assembling research done by historians. But for the Iraqi analysts, there is no historical baseline (that is, there is no classified historical study of Iraqi scientists). Or, if the project may be addressing a totally new issue (that is, if the scientist we are looking for is actually a Russian scientist recruited by the Iraqis). In this case, the project is truly "novel"—in the sense that they must look for unexpected relationships. It may be that the data were never collected, but if the data were contained in the dataset, it may not be amenable to straightforward analysis.

Data-mining is easy for known "bad guys" but not very good for identifying new ones—without a source somehow saying "this new guy is suspicious, and you should examine him." This is the true challenge that "massive" data presents—"How can we data-mine an existing dataset for new relationships between unknown entities?" But if the dataset does not even have a method to extract all the entities or a method to describe all the possible types of interactions between them, this is impossible.

A simple way of organizing data used by historians and other researchers—and indeed sometimes 8th graders—to solve this problem is the tried-and-true 3" by 5" index card (3x5 card). After the relevant documents are collected, the researcher uses the Table of Contents or Index to find and read the relevant sections—or sometimes just reads the entire document if the interactions have not been well defined—and writes down individual interactions as single sentences on 3x5 note cards (along with bibliographic reference data). Once all the current relevant documents are parsed this way, all the 3x5 cards are re-organized to follow threads of interactions that tell a story. Different cards arranged different ways could tell many stories off the same 3x5 card deck. The historian can then tell the story for the project at hand and save all the cards for later re-analysis. Often by following threads through the 3x5 card deck, "novel" relationships will emerge that allow telling unexpected stories.

In essence, relational databases are merely electronic 3x5 card decks. Relational databases have the advantage that once the individual interactions are entered, the electronic 3x5 cards can be arranged and re-arranged in many ways. But, both relational databases and 3x5 card decks are limited; it does not matter how elaborate the electronic interfaces and tools or how big and ornate the 3x5 card box, the ability to mine new data depends on the quality and number of "cards" that comprise the dataset.

IC Challenge: How can we rapidly build the huge relational datasets required for the wide range of problems needed to be analyzed by the IC? How may the historian or researcher be replaced by an electronic tool that can effectively read and understand language well enough to build an effective electronic "3x5 card" file?

The major problem in using the massive quantities available to the Community has less to do with the sheer magnitude of the data than the lack of historians to build a baseline of knowledge and the lack of librarians and curators to organize and tag the data for easy retrieval. We must reconcile ourselves to the fact that the Intelligence Community is unlikely to hire human historians, librarians and curators to support analysts in the way that other information-dependent organizations support their researchers. This means that we must develop methods to bypass the need for historians, librarians and curators by automating those functions, that is, developing computer tools for data archiving and retrieval.

Example 2 — The Submariner's Bearing-Only Targeting Problem

"Massive" data can also be data that contain more dimensions than can be handled by the available data collection, analysis, or representation tools.

Submariners deal with the problem of data dimensionality on a day-to-day basis. We can use a simple submarine bearings-only Time-Motion Analysis (TMA) to demonstrate that a dataset of only four data points can be too "massive" for the analyst to draw a meaningful answer if the methods by which the data were collected and analyzed did not account for the dimensionality of the problem.

In sub vs. sub encounters, the submariner usually uses passive sonar, which can only collect bearings to the target. Obtaining direct ranges requires using active sonar, which the submariner is loath to use because it gives away his presence. The passive sonar bearings are then plotted and used to analyze for the target's course, speed and range.

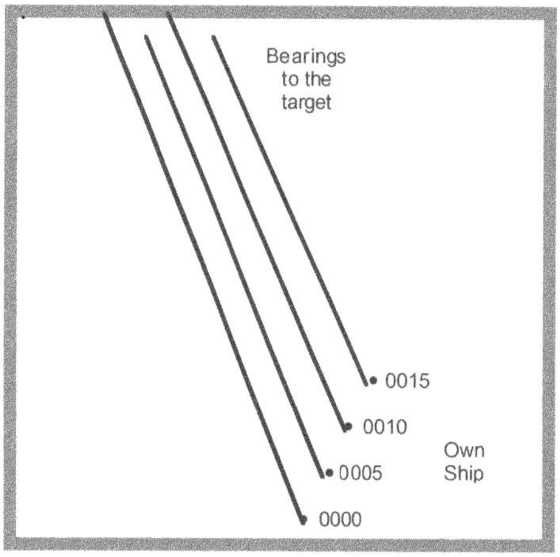

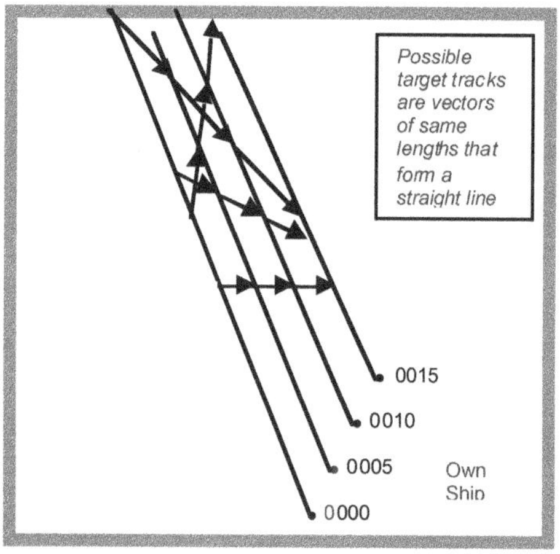

The submariner needs to know both where the target is now and also what its intentions are to be able to intercept it. Every submariner knows that a full target description contains four distinct parameters: (1) bearing, (2) range, (3) course, and (4) speed. Therefore, at least four observations are required to define all four. Using only bearings (as shown on the right), possible target tracks are the series of vectors between the observed bearings that define a straight line. Unfortunately, it can be shown mathematically that determination of the range depends indirectly on not only the target course vector but also the "own ship's" course vector. Accordingly, there are an infinite number of possible target descriptions using a set of plotted bearing lines if "own ship" remains on the same course.

That means that unless own ship maneuvers during the bearings-only approach, the dimensionality of the solution is greater than the dimensionality of the data and a target description solution is impossible!

Therefore, the submariner knows that the dataset required to solve the bearings-only TMA problem requires at least two observations on two different "own ship" courses. It is only after own-ship collects two bearings, maneuvers and collects two more bearings that a solution can be attempted (as shown below). This drives both the submariner's thinking toward data collection as well as his patience in knowing when a solution is possible.

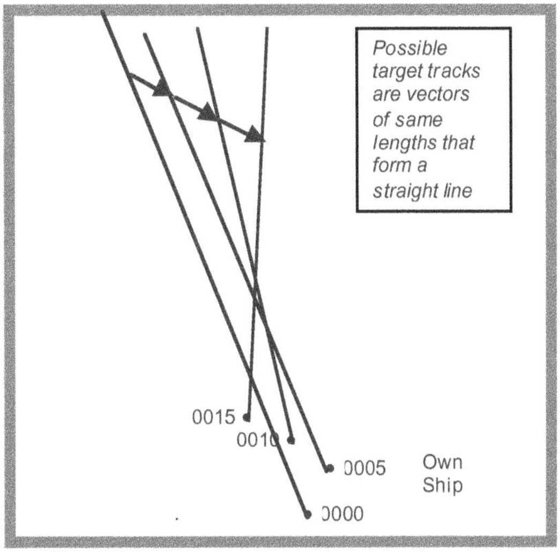

Like the submariner, the intelligence analyst needs to know a target's current location and its intentions—but the analyst's targets are much more complex. The simple submarine TMA problem indicates that in determining location and intentions a minimum amount of data *of the appropriate dimensionality* is required. Collection of the required data requires planning to ensure that the dimensionality of the data can support the dimensionality of the problem. Furthermore, data collection and analysis will require a certain amount of time.

History matters in determining intentions! One cannot know where a target is going unless we know where it has been. And the more complex the problem, the more history that must be collected and analyzed to construct a model that reflects both target current position and projected intentions.

Analytical methods depend on data that reflect the dimensionality of the problem. Collecting and analyzing massive amounts of data will not provide valid assessments if the dimensionality of the data does not reflect the dimensionality of the problem. Moreover, analytical methods are required to assess both current position and projected intentions.

Methodologies that hope to project target intentions into the future must be based on data collection for a longer time period into the past. In the current intelligence world, data cannot be used to build warning intelligence. To be able to provide tactical or strategic warning in a world of WMD and terrorism, we must begin to rebuild the Intelligence Community by:

- Moving beyond Newtonian thinking to use new analytical methods built on quantum thinking.
- Finding ways past our lack of historians, librarians, and curators to build new ways to assemble, catalog, and retrieve data.
- Moving beyond the 2-dimensional Newtonian world to build new methodologies built on quantum thinking that will allow us to think in multiple dimensions.

Only then can we move beyond Industrial-Age, Newtonian intelligence that considers only capability, to Information-Age intelligence that can consider both capability and intent.

Chapter 7

FROM CURRENT INTELLIGENCE TO STRATEGIC WARNING

> *Information-Age organizations needed to combat WMD and terrorism proliferation networks must be able to process intelligence and make decisions differently from Industrial-Age organizations in the Cold War. Using the Decision Cycle (or OODA Cycle) as a model for how organizations work suggests that the nature of the organization (network vs. hierarchy) is dependent on its goals and its environment. The ability to provide strategic warning requires that information flow within Intelligence Community must change by changing the way the organization processes information.*

More could be less if commanders cannot make sense of it. Even in 1991, when far less information streamed into Schwarzkopf's headquarters, it was difficult to separate out the best information, says former Marine lieutenant general Bernard Trainor. "It was like a fire hose coming out, and people were getting information of no interest or value to them, and information that was (of value) didn't get to them," says Trainor, co-author of *The General's War: The Inside Story of the Conflict in the Gulf*. "I don't think that has been solved."[24]

> The top worries in the minds of the men who will run the war with Iraq reflect the new face of warfare-information overload and a temptation to micromanage battles from their high-tech command center in Qatar.[25]

Information Overload is a new reality to the Intelligence Community. It used to be that intelligence reporting was very scarce and very dear. Imagine a World War II intelligence analyst ever saying, "I don't have time to read everything that comes across my desk." Yet, that is not unusual today as a massive quantity of data is deposited in databases around the IC, much of which is never read.

> On the afternoon of May 7, a Central Intelligence Agency (CIA) officer tried desperately to contact intelligence officials in Europe to alert them to the fact that the Yugoslavian military facility they had targeted was, in fact, located one block away from where NATO pilots were about to drop bombs. By the time his concerns could be registered, planes taking part

[24]Andrea Stone, "Battlefield Clearly Visible Far Behind the Lines," *USA Today*, 13 March 2003, 9A.

[25]Paul Martin, "Glut Of Data From Battlefield A New Command Problem," *Washington Times*, 19 March 2003, A12.

> in NATO's Operation Allied Force already were flying toward the target. When the smoke cleared the next morning, NATO awoke to the harsh reality that it had just bombed the Chinese embassy and killed three people. In his official explanation of the factors that contributed to the deadly mistake, CIA director George Tenet described a "severely flawed" target identification process made worse by the use of outdated maps and databases filled with erroneous information.[26]

After Sputnik and 9/11, the Intelligence Community has been frustrated by its inability to provide strategic or even tactical warning. And yet it has computer databases full of massive quantities of data.

> Today, the Defense Intelligence Agency is moving forward with a program that promises within the next five years to eliminate minor yet potentially deadly errors from proliferating throughout the intelligence community. Known as the Joint Intelligence Virtual Architecture (JIVA), the goal of the program is to help analysts overcome information overload by transforming the once ad hoc process of sharing critical intelligence data into a fully digitized, dynamic environment.[27]

The Intelligence Community has been building and rebuilding and pouring massive resources into solving "the database problem." Yet there appear to be very few signs of real progress. The databases do not seem to be sufficient to being converted into more valuable intelligence. Why not? Cynthia Grabo provides a clue...

> Intelligence is made up of many facets and types of information, some simple, and some complex. Some readily understood by non-experts, and some that require detailed research and analysis before they have meaning to users. If the sole function of intelligence was to compile "facts," there would be little need for analysts of any type. The intelligence process would consist almost entirely of collection of raw data which would be evaluated for accuracy but then passed on without further comment or analysis to the policy official.[28]

Current intelligence is different from tactical warning and strategic warning. As Ms. Grabo notes, the key to warning intelligence is not collection but rather

---

[26]Daniel Verton, *Federal Computer Week*, 18 October 1999. URL: www. fcw. com. Cited hereafter as Verton.

[27]Verton.

[28]Grabo, 133.

analysis. A bigger database full of massive quantities of data does not equate to better warning. Only better analysis and the ability to provide context can provide better warning.

We can only design better analysis by first understanding how we think and analyze. The problem is not how any one of us thinks but rather how to mobilize all the brainpower in the IC to be able to think as one. Before we can build databases that work, we must first understand the interplay of intelligence and operations in current organizations to understand what those databases can—and cannot—do.

Tradeoffs between Intelligence and Operations

Col John Boyd defined military decisionmaking by a "decision cycle," or "OODA Cycle," where decisionmakers **O**bserve, **O**rient, **D**ecide, and **A**ct. Thus a basic visualization of any military or political system is a timeline.

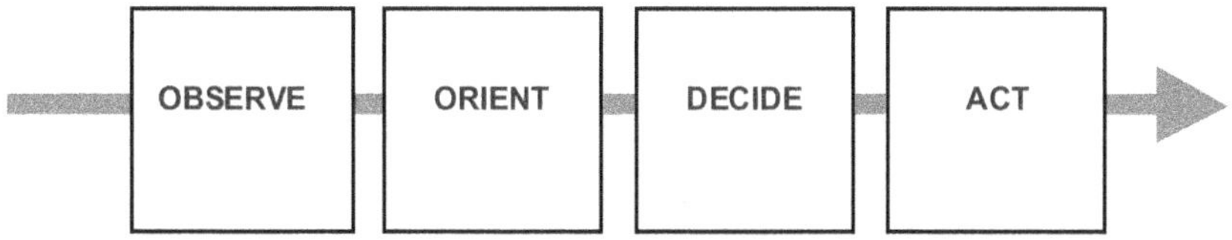

Each OODA Cycle can in itself be broken down into its component parts, each one of which is also an OODA cycle. For example, the D-Day invasion of Normandy hinged on the ability to launch the invasion force between several Atlantic storms. To do so required: observing weather in Iceland and in the Atlantic, orienting all the data on a weather map, deciding that it was time to go, and acting by launching the invasion force. But each one of those steps was itself an OODA cycle:

- The meteorologist "observing" in Iceland measured wind speed and barometric pressure with his instruments, oriented the marks on the instruments to numbers they represented, decided to send the readings to England, and acted by radioing the readings.
- The meteorologist "orienting" in England observed all the incoming radio messages with readings, oriented them on a weather map, decided what they meant, and acted by briefing General Eisenhower that the time was right.

- The "decisionmaker" General Eisenhower, observed the weather brief, oriented the information to his internal timeline and experience, decided that the time was right, and acted by saying, "Let's go."
- All the "actors" and forces in the invasion force observed the order from Eisenhower, oriented it against their Op-order, decided it was time, and acted in unison to invade.

In each of these nested OODA Cycles there is a plan—a systematic series of steps from conception (of what needs to be done) through maturity (of actually getting it done).

As organizations evolve from loose confederations to integrated systems of systems, the components of the organization redefine their roles: going from working in parallel to working as an integrated team. The increasing demands of the Information Age for quality intelligence and warning analysis require that the Intelligence Community clearly define the roles of its component agencies to do the most with its most scarce asset—its analysts.

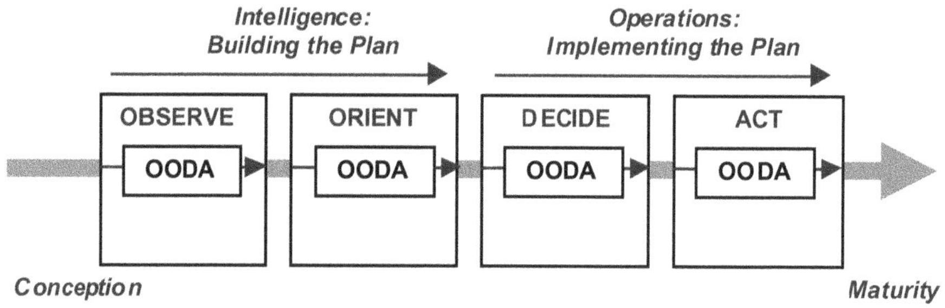

The Evolution of Organizations through Integration of Decision Cycles

The evolution of complex systems goes through a definable series of steps as new levels of complexity emerge. The first step is the formation of a new unit where before there was only a set of unlinked individuals.

The resulting loosely linked organization, which we will call a network, is linked by common interests. All the individuals (be they organisms, groups of organisms, or organizations) share their observations and orientations (assessments of those observations) but reserve the right to decide and act on their own. A biological example is a colony of bacteria, and a social example is a commune. Even though decisions are made individually, if all the members of a network reach a consensus, the combination of all the individual actions will be much stronger than the sum of the parts: anthrax or botulinum bacteria can collectively kill an infected person by all secreting toxin where only one or a few could not; sharing a common well in a commune benefits all—even if everyone uses an individual bucket. A coalition of states that fights a common foe—even if their war fronts are totally unlinked—can provide for a common defense much more effectively than the individual countries acting on their own.

Often organizations continue to evolve beyond networks to provide for a better mechanism to insure coordinated action.

All biological systems are defined by four characteristic processes, which include the ability to: (1) extract and store energy from the environment, (2) sense and respond to the environment, (3) reproduce, and (4) evolve. The Decision Cycle or OODA Cycle is just another way of defining the second of these processes—the ability to sense and respond to the environment.

In the OODA or Decision Cycle, the first two steps—observation and orientation—are what we commonly call intelligence. An individual's or organization's ability to make the best possible decision is directly dependent on both the quality of its observations of the world and its assessments of what those observations mean. The orientation step is a comparison of the input observations against an internal map or model of the world whereby the "orienter" or analyst can define its own position in the world and define possible actions by displaying options on the internal map and projecting whether they will lead to "rocks and shoals" or to a "safe harbor."

In the OODA or Decision Cycle, the second two steps—decision and action—are what we commonly called operations. Once all the possible options are laid out on the internal map and assessments of their strengths and weaknesses are made, a decision is made to take the best possible action. The more coordinated the parts of the organism or organization are in carrying out that action, the more effective that action will be.

Networks have an advantage over groups of unlinked individuals in that the individuals in the network can share their observations and assessments. This makes the network much more informed because the individuals can share not only observations of others who might be able to see farther or hear better, but also assessments of dangers or possible actions from those who might have a more refined map or model.

The inability for networks to be able to provide mechanisms for coherent decisionmaking or coordinated operations usually means that networks evolve toward a second kind of organization which we will call a hierarchy. In a hierarchy individuals subordinate their decisionmaking role to a single leader. This makes the hierarchy much more efficient because the individuals can work cooperatively toward the same goals based on the decisions of the leader.

Networks and hierarchies have inherent advantages over each other, but which is best? Just as chemists use ideal compounds—the ideal gas and the perfect crystal—we can compare a perfect network and perfect hierarchy to understand how they work. Whenever we cannot imagine a "perfect" network or hierarchy, we can consider the closest real-world examples: a commune is almost a pure network while Stalin's USSR or the Saddam Hussein's Iraq approached pure hierarchies.

Networks versus Hierarchies—Informed Inaction versus Uninformed Action

The network has the advantage over the hierarchy in that the observing and orienting process is distributed over the entire organization—which means that it can bring all the observational and assessment skills of every individual to bear on any problem. The wide-open lines of communication in the network make for effectiveness in sensing the world and orienting its place in that environment. However, since organizational operations must be accomplished by consensus, the network is inefficient in decisionmaking or acting. The network is thoughtful and effective but slow and inefficient. In short, a network is characterized by informed inaction.

The hierarchy has the advantage over the network in that the decisionmaking is concentrated in a single individual, which means that there will always be unanimity in actions because all individuals are following orders of the leader. The restricted lines of communication in the hierarchy make for efficiency in operations. However, since all the orienting processes are also concentrated in a single individual, the hierarchy is only as smart as its leader. The hierarchy is fast and efficient but superficial and often ineffective. In short, a hierarchy is characterized by uninformed action.

But which is better—a network or a hierarchy? It all depends... For both organisms and organizations, the "better" solution is the one that leads to organismal or organizational survival. The alternative is extinction or regime change.

The key to any Decision Cycle is the ability to formulate and implement a plan of action that will be the best response to the environment on the basis of all available observed data. And there will always be three kinds of tradeoffs required for any organism or organization: (1) the today or tomorrow tradeoff, (2) the guns or butter tradeoff, and (3) the intelligence or operations tradeoff.

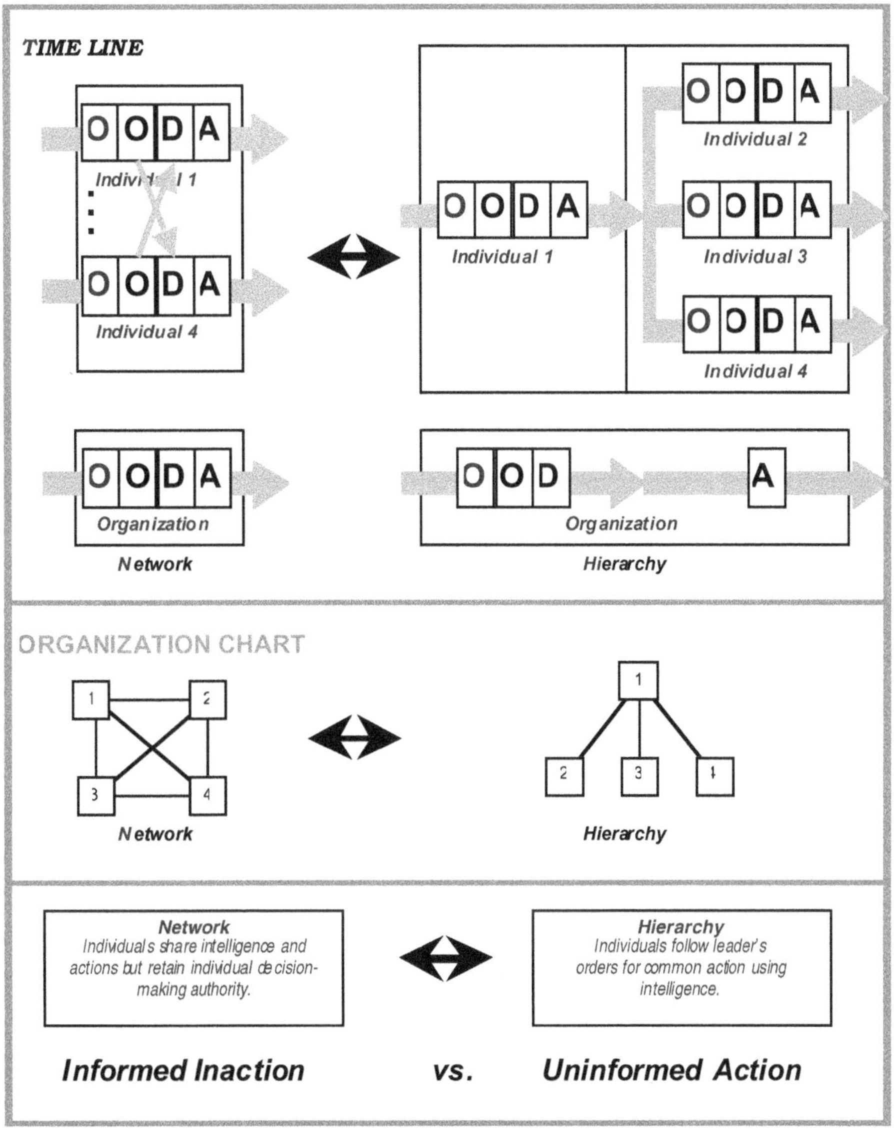

The present versus future tradeoff comes from the dichotomy between the need of the organism or organization to extract and store energy from the environment and the need to reproduce. The more resources put away for another day the better the organism or organization can exploit tomorrow's environment, whatever that may be. However, the more resources that can be used today—to act or to reproduce—the better the organism can most efficiently exploit today's environment. In a world of limited resources, an organism or organization is always faced with the choice, "Do I use my resources today or save them for tomorrow?"

The guns or butter tradeoff comes from the dichotomy between the need of the organism or organization to sense and respond to the environment and the need to reproduce. The more resources put into systems that allow efficient ability to maintain today's organism or organization—the guns that allow defense from environmental threats—the better the existing organism or organization can survive today. However, the more resources put into systems that allow effective ability to build tomorrow's progeny organism or organization—the "butter" to build new infrastructure—the better the progeny of the organism or organization will be able to survive tomorrow. In a world of limited resources, an organism or organization is always faced with the choice, "Do I use my resources to make guns or butter?"

The intelligence or operations tradeoff comes from the dichotomy between the need of the organism or organization to be able to effectively sense (observe and orient) and to efficiently respond (decide and act). The more resources an organism or organization can use to observe the world in fine detail in many ways and integrate those observations into contingency plans for a wide variety of environments, the better it can make informed decisions. However, the more resources an organism or organization can use to make rapid decisions and conform coordinated actions, the better it can exploit the environment. In a world of limited resources, an organism or organization is always faced with the choice, "Do I use my resources for better intelligence or for more efficient operations?" This ultimately translates into "Do I organize myself into a network or into a hierarchy?"

The best kind of organization in any case is the one that can best complete Decision Cycles that address the three tradeoffs... Today or tomorrow? Guns or butter? Intelligence or operations?

As we will see shortly, the critical point in any Decision Cycle is the transition from orienting to decisionmaking. This depends on both an accurate and complete internal map/model of the world and the ability to provide actionable options for all foreseeable futures. An organization that can build and implement the most effective and efficient plan will be the one that will prevail.

And we will see that the choices made by the organism or organization not only determine how much of its resources to allocate to intelligence but also what kind of intelligence to value most... current intelligence, tactical warning, or strategic warning.

In times of stasis or equilibrium—when tomorrow's world will be the same as today's—the hierarchy is better. And in times of stasis or equilibrium only current intelligence is needed.

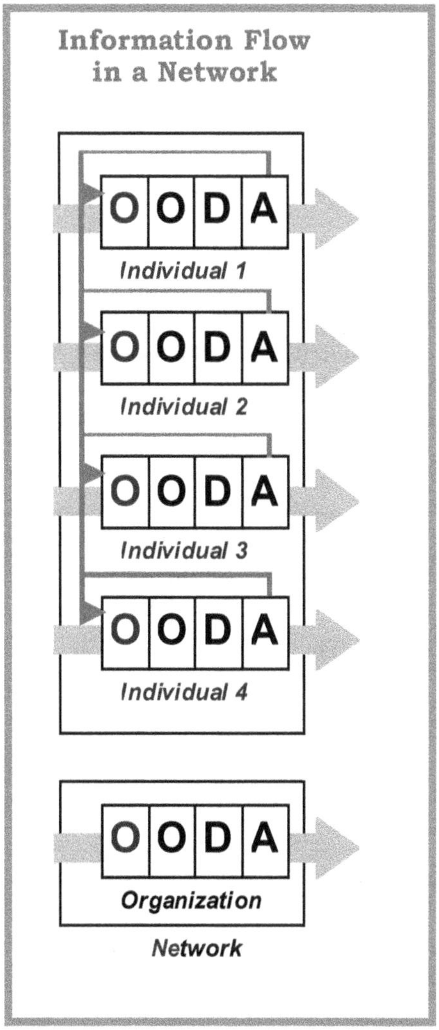

The first possibility is that the world can be modeled as continuous and single-valued; that is, changes will happen only incrementally and there is only one possible output for any given input. As we have seen, these are the conditions under which Newtonian models apply, which are inherently two-player zero-sum-games. If an organism or organization can approximate its world as a two-player zero-sum-game *and* can assume that the other player will not change the way it is playing the game, the complementarity conditions for Newtonian thinking apply, and a hierarchy will provide the best solution to the three tradeoffs.

Guns or butter? In a world where threats are well defined and are not expected to change markedly in capability or intent, a simple Newtonian model can be made for the threats, especially when there is only a single major threat. Once that model is made, it is a two-player zero-sum-game which can—after enough historical data points have been collected to validate it—be converted into a "function" at which point the future can be predicted rather well. Once an answer is obtained, be it "butter now," "guns now," or "some mixture of guns and butter now," a single plan can be built for the organization. At that point, the decision is easy and all possible resources should concentrate on implementing the plan. Since hierarchies are best at operations, a hierarchy is the best choice.

Today or tomorrow? If a Newtonian model applies today, since it is continuous and single-valued, it will change only incrementally tomorrow. If the plan can account for any deviations from equilibrium, such as an incrementally growing arms race, the model will not change nor must the plan. Since tomorrow's plan will then look much like today's, the plan should be made to optimize the choice of guns or butter for today—neglecting tomorrow because tomorrow will not change enough to change the plan. Once the plan has been made, the hierarchy will implement it best.

Intelligence or operations? Once the plan is made in a static world using a Newtonian model, intelligence is only needed to check the plan to look for minor deviations that need to be corrected. Therefore, under such conditions, the bulk of an organism's or organization's resources should be dedicated to operations. In a static world, current intelligence is most critical to provide constant but rather easily assessed feedback to ensure that things are going according to the plan.

In summary:

- When the world is not changing and a plan has already been made, it is best to maximize resources used for operations to implement that plan. A hierarchy is best to do so.
- The organization in a static world only needs enough intelligence resources to monitor that the plan is being implemented properly.
- Current intelligence provides data to assess that the current plan is satisfactory for current operations.
- In a static world, current intelligence is all that is needed.

In times of change— when tomorrow's world will be incrementally different from today's—a command network, an organization that balances a network and a hierarchy, is best. And in times of incremental change tactical warning becomes most important.

The second possibility is that of a two player model, quantum and multi-state. Here there are only two players in the game but the other player will make decisions during the course of the game. Since Newtonian models cannot account for decisionmaking, these are conditions that transcend Newtonian models even if they are two-player zero-sum-games. In a world where the adversary is making decisions, as in changing its plans, but those decisions are predictable, the organization can include contingency plans within its overall plan. For example, the organization has assessed that the adversary will begin hostilities and has structured itself to defeat the adversary when the attack does come. Thus a plan was constructed that accounts for operations prior to hostile action and operations during hostile action. A hybrid organization, which we will call a command network, provides the best solution to the three tradeoffs under these conditions.

Guns or butter? Since the adversary's overall plan—hostile action—is assessed, the plan has already accounted for a current mix of guns and butter. Therefore, resources are best allocated toward implementing the plan; this is best done by a hierarchy. However, during the time period prior to the commencement of hostilities, tactical warning is needed to provide decision-makers options on how best to react to the commencement of hostilities. Therefore, a large enough intelligence network must be built into the organization to provide good prospects for tactical warning.

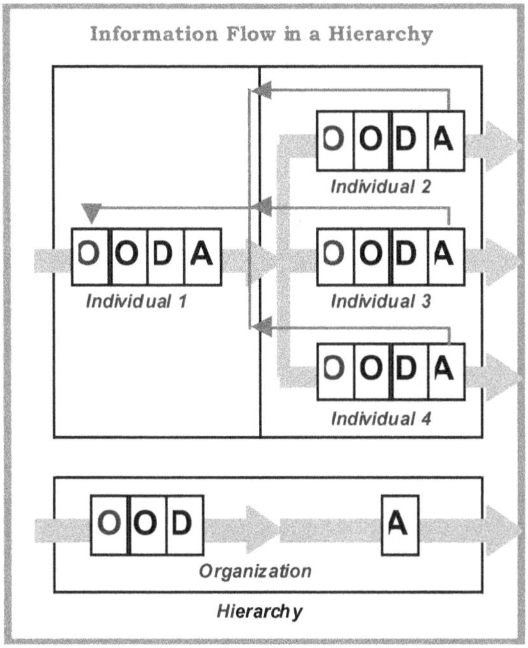

Today or tomorrow? In this context, today or tomorrow is relevant mainly to the moment that hostilities begin. Therefore, the plan needs to consider multiple contingencies that include alternative actions dependent on when and where hostilities commence as well as the possibility of pre-emptive strike as an option within the plan. However, under these conditions, all planning becomes tactical because plans are made for allocation of current resources decided in the overall plan.

Intelligence or operations? Under these conditions, the organization must be flexible. Since a war is imminent, the organization must be set up as a hierarchy which is most effective once the war starts—at which point the situation reverts to a two-player-zero-sum game with no change in opponent plans (as long as the war is on) as described above. However, until hostilities begin (or if the opponent makes significant tactical changes in plan during the war), the organization must have the ability to provide tactical warning. During this pre-war phase at least, an intelligence infrastructure must be fielded to at least answer the tactical questions of when and where the opponent will attack. Thus, an intelligence network must be built which functions as closely as possible to a pure network to provide the best intelligence, but within a hierarchical framework to be able to support decisions and actions in support of the plan.

In summary:

- When the world will change in a predictable way, i.e., beginning hostilities, and a plan has already been made, it is best to maximize resources for operations to implement that plan but still providing enough intelligence assets to be able to implement the contingencies of the plan most effectively. The best organization is a command network which is set up as a hierarchy but which can operate like a network prior to decision-points in the plan.
- Tactical warning provides data to assess when contingencies within the current plan must be accounted for to support current and future operations.
- In a predictably changing world, tactical warning is needed.

In paradigm shifts, when the assumptions in tomorrow's thinking will be backward from today's, a network is better. And in paradigm shifts strategic warning becomes most important.

The third possibility is that the world can be modeled as a quantum phenomenon that is multi-state and multi-player; that is, changes will happen in steps, there is more than one possible output for any given input, and one must account for the actions of multiple players. These are conditions that transcend both Newtonian models and two-player zero-sum-games. Here the organism or organization needs to model the world as a multi-player non-zero-sum-game *and* must assume that the other players will make decisions during the course of the game being played. In the worst-case scenario, all the multiple players make plans independently based on their own guns-or-butter, today-or-tomorrow, and intelligence-or-operations tradeoffs, and the organization must build plans from intelligence and implement them knowing that all the other players are doing the same simultaneously.

Guns or butter? In a world of constant, quantum change, the organization is only as strong as its infrastructure, and an infrastructure which can respond to a wide variety of conditions will be best. Since war is only one of many possible futures in such a world, the organization that can maximize its ability to build a diverse infrastructure will be most effective. Thus under these conditions the more "butter" of the most possible kinds the better, and the closer the organization can be to a network of autonomous diverse parts, the better.

Today or tomorrow? In a world of constant, quantum change, tomorrow will be different from today. Therefore, any plans for today will become obsolete almost instantaneously. A network is needed to be able to plan for the most plausible contingencies.

Intelligence or operations? In a world of constant, quantum change, the network is the key, and the better intelligence the organization has, the better it can react to the constantly changing world. Besides, a large and costly infrastructure required to implement a long-range plan will likely become obsolete before it is ever used. Thus, the best intelligence in such an environment is one that can correctly predict far enough into the future to provide decisionmakers with the best plan that accounts for not only changes in adversary plans but also the ability for the organization to be able to reallocate its resources *before* the world changes. When there are multiple kinds of butter and guns—any one of which could be the most effective tomorrow—the organization that can best reallocate its resources will be most effective. Under these conditions, strategic warning becomes most important.

In summary:

- When the world will change constantly in a complex way, with many players constantly building and implementing plans, it is best to maximize resources for intelligence to be able to effectively build new plans to reallocate resources. The best organization is a network.
- Strategic warning provides data to assess when new plans must be built in support of current and future operations.
- In a constantly changing, complex world, strategic warning is the variety needed.

Is a network or hierarchy better? It all depends. Networks are best at making plans. Networks provide the best intelligence but cannot act in a concerted manner. Hierarchies are best at implementing plans. Hierarchies can act quickly and efficiently but are flying blind most of the time.

In a static world, a hierarchy is better because making plans in that environment is simple, and the organization can marshal its resources to implement the plan.

In a changing world, a network is better because making plans in that environment is difficult, and the organization needs to expend resources making contingency plans... the more complex the changing world, the more complex the plans need to be.

If change is small and can be neglected, the organization can make a simple plan and stick with it. Only current intelligence is required to monitor the progress of that plan. If change is small and predictable, the organization needs to make a plan with contingencies and look for indicators of that change to decide which contingencies to implement. Tactical warning is needed to provide those indicators. BUT...

If change is constant and too great to account for all possible contingencies in a single plan, no matter how complex the plan is, the organization must be able to build a new plan even while it is executing the old. That is what strategic warning is all about.

Current U.S. military and IC organizations were built to fight Industrial-Age wars. In the Industrial Age only current intelligence and tactical warning were required because strategic warning could be done by the decisionmakers themselves without any additional help from the IC:

- The Japanese bombing Pearl Harbor signaled a beginning of hostilities. FDR could come up with a strategic plan immediately to reallocate U.S. resources from butter to guns.
- The launching of Sputnik signaled the beginning of a new era. Eisenhower and the nation could immediately come up with a new strategic plan to reallocate U.S. resources from just butter to guns plus butter — and a standing "strategic" force to be on call for instant reaction to any Soviet attack. But once the new strategic plan was in place and all the contingencies of the plan fleshed out, the U.S. only needed tactical warning thereafter to assess and provide guidance at the decision-points in the plan.

But 9/11 changed all that. In a world where multiple players are building WMD and terrorists can attack anywhere at any time, how do we build a plan to counter WMD and terrorism? That requires strategic warning, and it appears that strategic warning is impossible in a constantly changing multi-player world.

Therefore, we must begin to do the impossible... Build an IC organization that can provide strategic warning in a world of WMD and terrorism.

From the Industrial Age to the Information Age–A New Balance between Intelligence and Operations

The Decision Cycle is curious in that it is advantageous to remain in the intelligence half (Observe and Orient) for as long as possible but implement the operations half (Decide and Act) as quickly as possible. Building a plan is best done with the maximum amount of information possible, so when an organization is in the intelligence half of an OODA Cycle it tends to stay there as long as possible.

However, once a decision is made and a plan is executed, it is advantageous to complete the plan as fast as possible because during the operations half of the cycle the organization is essentially flying blind.

One of the basic lessons of Decision Cycles is that the organization that can get "inside the adversary's decision loop" will prevail. In essence, if the organization can build a plan based on current assessments of the adversary and the world and complete that plan faster than the adversary, it will get the advantage of moving to the next Decision Cycle ahead of the adversary and be able construct a new and better plan that accounts for everything that has occurred during the current cycle. Feedback is possible during a Decision Cycle to allow monitoring to keep the plan on track or to provide for contingency decisions programmed into the plan, but it is only by going to the next Decision Cycle that the organization has a clean slate to build a new plan from scratch—one that can account for everything that happened during the current cycle.

Both current intelligence and tactical warning are reactive. They assume an organizational plan that is in place and being executed and looks for indicators that the plan is still on track or that contingencies—decision-points—in the plan

Information Flow in a Real-world Organization

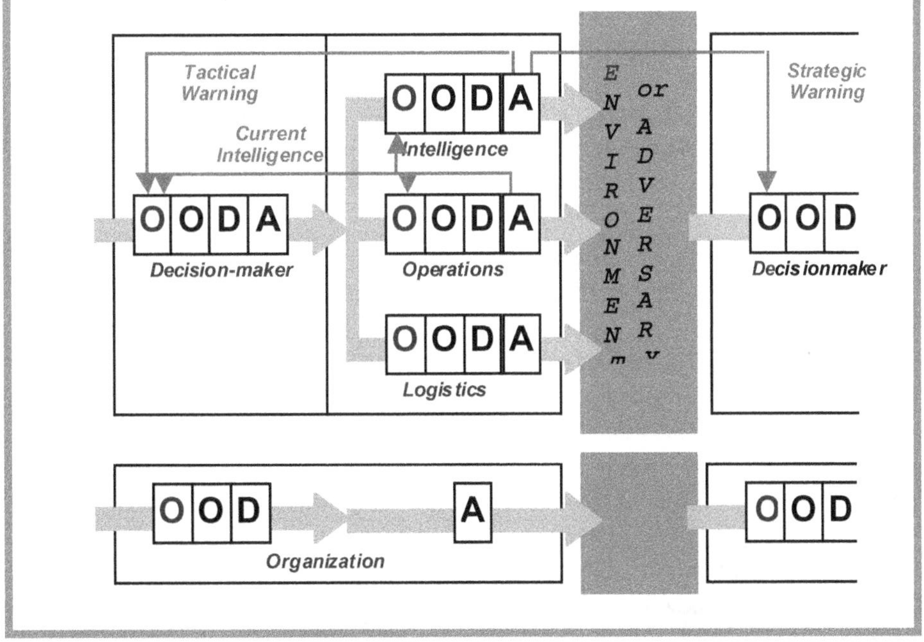

have been reached. "If they do A, then we'll do Y, but if they do B, then we'll do Z." In either of these modes, the decisionmakers drive intelligence. They already have a plan, and intelligence provides a feedback loop to monitor that plan. Therefore, decisionmakers drive current intelligence and tactical warning by defining the requirements of their *current* plan.

Strategic warning is proactive. It assumes that when the current organizational plan runs its course, the world will be different and that the new plan must reallocate current resources to implement it. Any complex plan takes time to implement and complete, and once a decision is made to implement a plan, it is usually more effective to complete that plan than stop and redraw another. Strategic warning provides inputs to plan for the *next* Decision Cycle. Therefore, strategic warning must ultimately be driven by analysts.

But it's even more difficult than that... True strategic warning needs to plan ahead not only into the *next* Decision Cycle but the Decision Cycle *beyond* that!

> In general—if it is possible to generalize on this—the policy official is probably most receptive to early, albeit tenuous, warning in cases where he can take some preliminary action, such as some diplomatic initiative, without incurring any significant risk or major commitment of resources. He is not likely to be so responsive if he has to undertake a redeployment of military forces or a call-up of reservists, particularly if he believes that the threat is not imminent or that action on our part could lead to military reaction by the adversary and an escalation of the situation. And he probably will not wish to be "warned" about potential dangers which still appear remote and which might require a major change of recently established national policy.[29]

Providing adequate strategic warning requires first recognizing that the current organization has not allocated its resources properly to react to the environment or threat and then requires formulating a plan to rebuild the organization to properly react to that environment or threat. It's not good enough for the strategic analyst to say, "We cannot meet the threat with our current organization and resources." The strategic analyst must also provide a *plan* for the next *two* Decision Cycles: the first plan is for an infrastructure OODA cycle that details the reallocation of resources and new organizations to manage what must *be built*; and the second plan is an operational OODA cycle that details the actions of the new organization using its new resources to respond to the environment or threat that will exist *after* new infrastructure is in place.

---

[29] Grabo, 143.

Thus, strategic warning must entail a thorough understanding not only of the adversary and how his decisions will affect changes that cannot be properly countered by today's infrastructure, but also an understanding of the analyst's own organization and the possible decisions it can make to reorganize its own infrastructure. Current intelligence provides feedback on how the current plan is going. Tactical intelligence provides feedback on how to implement a contingency plan within the current plan to account for new intelligence on the adversary or environment. Strategic intelligence must provide "feed-forward" on how to build a new plan: first a plan on how to reallocate current resources into a new infrastructure, then a plan on how to use that new infrastructure in responding to the adversary and environment. "Warning does not exist until it has been conveyed to the policymaker, and he must know that he has been warned."[30]

To rebuild the IC from its Industrial-age organization to a new Information-age organization we must begin with a new set of assumptions:

- In the Industrial-age action was the key to success. In the Information Age orienting will be the key to success.
- Action depended on the soldier. Orienting depends on the analyst.
- Action is best implemented by a hierarchy. Orienting is best implemented by a network.
- Action is served by current intelligence and tactical warning to insure the success of the current Decision Cycle. Orienting is best served by strategic warning to insure the success of the next Decision Cycle... and the one beyond that.

Current intelligence and tactical warning tells the decisionmaker what he *wants* to know. Strategic warning tells the decisionmaker what he *needs* to know.

---

[30]Grabo, 14.

Chapter 8

MODELING THE DECISION CYCLE

Biological Systems are defined by what they do rather than what they are. Dynamic models for biological systems including organisms and organizations can be built using the Decision Cycle or OODA Cycle developed by Col John Boyd.

Amateurs talk tactics. Professionals talk logistics.
Old Military Aphorism

How do we get there from here? With all the talk about "the database problem" or "systems of systems," is the world becoming too complex for the human brain to comprehend? I suggest that the world only seems that complex because we are basing our worldview and thought processes on what we learned in school...based on Newtonian Science.

Newtonian Science is based on the notion of understanding the physical universe. There has been much thought and discussion to step beyond Newton to build what is been termed "chaos theory" or "complexity theory." But ultimately, the current notions of complexity science have failed because they are based on Newtonian assumptions...half-a-honeybee...functions with no history...and most importantly no decisionmaking. Therein lies the problem.

Decisions are most usefully depicted as quantal and multi-state. One can start with A and get either B or C, dependent on the environment. Therefore any modeling of a decisionmaking system based on the Newtonian assumptions that the world is continuous and single-valued is inherently flawed and misleading.

To model a world based on the Decision Cycle one needs to start with a set of assumptions that recognizes decisions.

Therefore, we need to look more closely at the Decision Cycle and see where the complementarity principle applies; that is, where our Industrial Age, Newtonian assumptions approximate the real world and where they are woefully inadequate.

If we redraw the Decision Cycle the way it works in an organization, we can see not only why Newtonian thinking is limited for modeling the cycle but also why current technology-based methods to improve the intelligence process have failed.

The Decision Cycle exists not only in the physical world but also in the cognitive or organizational world and therefore transcends Newtonian thinking. In the Observation step of the cycle, the observer interacts directly with the physical world, performs measurements or senses physical entities, then converts the physical reality into a symbolic representation of that reality. The meteorologist in Iceland in support of D-Day measured wind direction and speed, and barometric pressure but passed the data he collected in symbolic format (305o@25kt/28.5"Hg). The symbolic data was then passed to the meteorologist in England who plotted all the symbols on a map, which is itself a symbolic representation of the physical world. He then oriented and presented all the data on the weather map to General Eisenhower who decided on the best plan based on the symbolic worldview. Eisenhower then passed the decision in symbolic form, "Let's go," and finally the operational part of the organization took actions in the physical world which affected physical entities (the German Army or the environment). The input Observation and the output Action relate the organizational world to the physical world, but the Orienting and Decisionmaking steps exist totally in an organizational cognitive world based on totally non-Newtonian symbolic data, maps, plans, decisions, and orders.

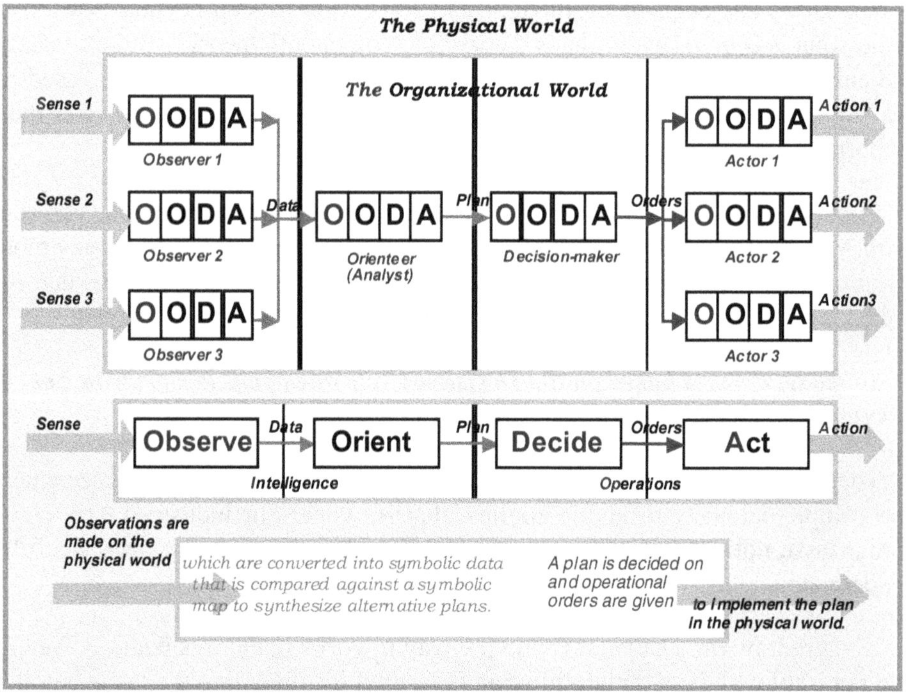

Efforts to date to use information technology have heavily concentrated on the Newtonian fringes of the Decision Cycle; that is, the parts of the Observation and Action steps that occur in the physical world. Thus we built physical systems to answer questions about physical systems. How do we build bigger and better sensors to load more data into databases? How can we speed up our ability to pass orders to allow our operating forces to target faster? But Newton cannot help us with orienting and decisionmaking because both only exist in the cognitive organizational world.

Both the Observer and Actor *do* things, and technology based on physical models can help them *do* things faster or farther or stronger. Industrial-Age technology provided machine-aided methods for the Observation and Action steps of the Decision Cycle in which the organization interacts with the physical world.

Both the Orienter and Decisionmaker *think* things, and technology based on biological or cognitive models can help them *think* more effectively. Information-Age technology will ultimately allow computer-aided methods for the Orienting and Decisionmaking steps of the Decision Cycle in which the organization interacts within itself cognitively.

The core of the Decision Cycle is making and implementing a plan.

Orienting compares symbolic representations of the physical world against a symbolic representation of the world—usually called a map—and synthesizes plans.

Decisionmaking selects which plan to implement.

The key to Information-Age Intelligence and strategic warning is in understanding how both our organization and an adversary's organization make plans and in how we can make our plans better than their plans.

- Better operations required more efficient machines.
- Better plans require more effective thinking.

In a rapidly changing world the key is to be able to build an organization that can respond most effectively to the new environment. This entails a strategic plan that must span two Decision Cycles: in a Logistics Cycle a plan is formulated and implemented to reallocate resources to build a new infrastructure, that is, a plan to change from "butter to guns" by building a wartime economy; in the Operational Cycle a plan is formulated to employ the new infrastructure to respond to the environment in a new way, that is, to actually fight the war.

A journey of a thousand miles begins with a single step.
Chinese Proverb

The single step I hope to accomplish is to be able to build a plan on how we can build better plans through better strategic intelligence using Information-Age technology.

Lessons Learned are Better than Any Plan

A problem with evaluating plans is that one cannot truly tell how good a plan is until it is actually implemented. It did not matter how complex or exciting all the turn-of-the-century plans were for flying machines, the proof of the Wright brothers' plan was that their aircraft actually got off the ground and flew. In the age of "vaporware" where PowerPoint slides of systems on the drawing board are touted as the wave of the future, the proof is in the product. If a plan for better intelligence is really a better plan, then one should be able to demonstrate intelligence products based on that plan.

Accordingly, I will demonstrate by "lessons learned" from a conceptual prototype that I have been building in DIA's Biological Warfare Assessments Divisions along with much help from many members of the IC. There are two sections to my strategic plan for Information-age intelligence: (1) The **Methods** Section details a conceptual model for computer-aided multidimensional strategic analysis both of target nations and terrorist groups and of the IC itself to use as a basis for reorienting current thinking and current organizational dynamics to produce better intelligence—especially strategic warning; (2) The **Case Studies** detail several implementations of that plan to demonstrate how the new methodology can provide better intelligence, not only to understand the adversary's capabilities but intent as well.

If you think systematically and logically, read on directly… But if you're thinking "Show me," please read the case studies first, and if you feel you know more about WMD programs and how to deal with them than you have before, then come back and read about how that was done.

Assumptions—From Industrial-Age Tinkering to Information-Age Thinking

The methodology to model organizational decisionmaking cannot be built in a Newtonian world and must be built on quantum assumptions. Accordingly, before I begin to describe the methodology, let me briefly reiterate my change *from* the Industrial-Age assumptions I am discarding *to* the Information-Age assumptions I will use.

From

Bigger Faster Technology — The key player on the battlefield is the guy with his finger on the ICBM launch button. IMINT and MASINT are the keys to Industrial-Age targeting

To

Smarter Thinking — The key player on the battlefield is the guy on horseback with the binoculars, GPS, and laser-pointer. HUMINT is the key to Information-Age targeting. History Matters.

From

Fighting against Technologies — Shoot them all, and you'll get the one you want.

To

Out-Thinking Decisionmakers — Only shoot the ones who have decided to shoot you.

From

I can project the future from today's function. Instantaneous data mean instantaneous decisions.

To

I can project the future only by knowing the past. History Matters!

From

Targeting Objects — It is "Us" versus "Them," and the World is bipolar. For analysis, one size fits all.

To

Targeting Individuals — It's a multi-polar world where every nation, organization, and individual has distinct goals and decisionmaking processes to reach those goals. For analysis, it all depends; context is critical.

From

Assessment of capabilities built on understanding and identifying things—weapons and the facilities that make them.

To

Assessment of intent built on understanding people and the organizations, nations, and cultures they build—for it is people who build WMD.

From

Intelligence that is reactive built on current intelligence and tactical warning.

To

Intelligence that is proactive built on strategic warning.

And finally

True strategic warning needs to plan ahead not only into the next Decision Cycle but the Decision Cycle *beyond* that!

From Thinking Tactically to Thinking Strategically

To transcend Newtonian models of the world, we need to begin to build new models for the world that encompass not only the physical world but the cognitive organizational world as well.

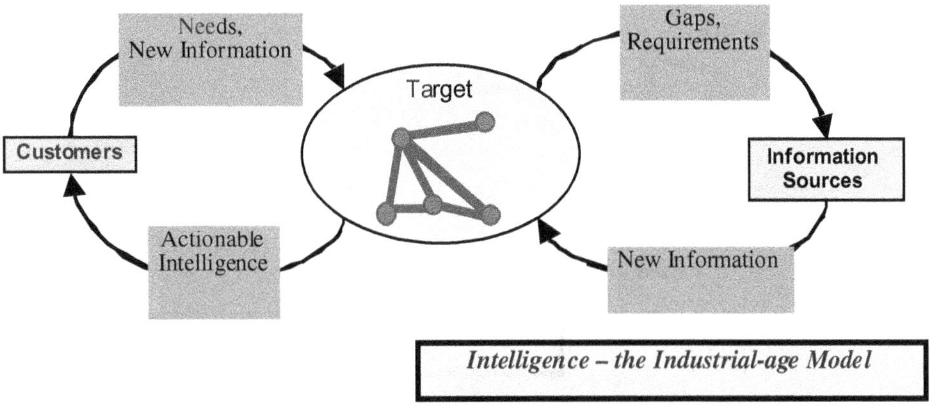

The Intelligence Cycle — Now[31]

Current thinking in the IC is linear—both in modeling the adversary and in the model by which the IC collects, collates, analyzes, and presents finished intelligence to the customer. As indicated by Robert Clark,[32] we need to reorient our thinking to account for the non-linear network aspects of the entire process. This includes three parts: modeling the target or adversary, modeling ourselves, and modeling how we model. Any new methodology for the Information Age must

[31] Robert M. Clark, Model-Based Predictive Techniques, Lecture at the National Security Agency, 2001.

[32] Clark.

address all three as well as providing mechanisms to integrate them into a coherent whole.

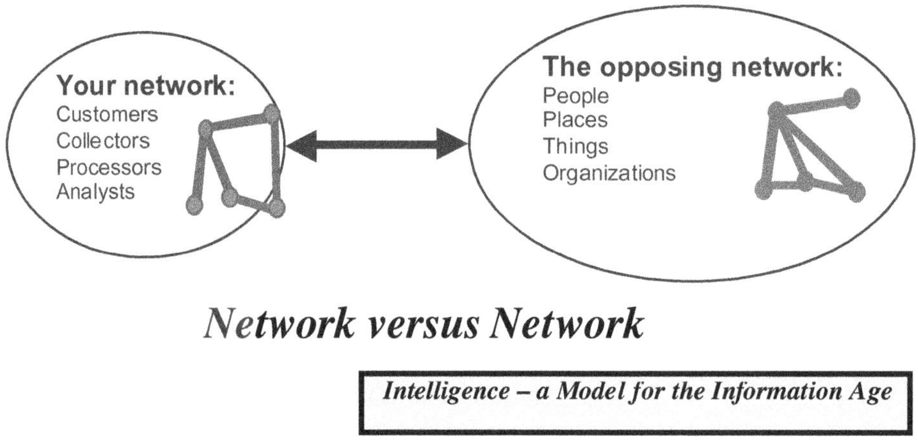

The Intelligence Cycle — Future[33]

Modeling the Target: How Do We Find Out the Adversary's Strategic Plan?

> It is the history of warfare, and of warning, that the extraordinary buildup of military force or capability is often the single most important and valid indication of intent.[34]

After 9/11, "extraordinary" is a single WMD or terrorist act. This could be a single fermenter and crop duster or could be a single hijacked airliner. Unfortunately, the IC now must be able to understand and model both the capability and intent prior to a single "extraordinary" event...in essence to predict the "extraordinary" by only being able to know the "ordinary."

> The precept that intelligence properly deals only with, or should only assess, capabilities derives, of course, from the requirements of the field commander. Confronted with military forces which may attack him or which he is preparing to attack, it is essential that the commander have the most accurate possible assessment of the capabilities

---

[33] Clark.

[34] Grabo, 22.

> of enemy forces and that he prepare his defenses or plan his offense against what the enemy is capable of doing rather than attempting to guess what he might do.[35]

The primary concern of the warfighter is the capabilities of the adversary. This is tactical intelligence.

> The validity of this concept, however, does not mean that intelligence at the national and strategic level should be confined to the assessment of capabilities. For the fact is that intelligence at all levels, but particularly that which is prepared for the guidance of policy officials, is expected to deal with the question of intentions.[36]

The primary concern of the policymaker is the "question of intentions." This is the realm of strategic intelligence.

When dealing with current intelligence, tactical intelligence, and strategic intelligence, the IC is currently the weakest in providing strategic intelligence. But in the world of WMD and terrorism, that must become our strength. I suggest the first step in that process is to mirror-image the adversary in a single aspect of modeling that we can exploit to turn a major weakness into a major strength. As indicated above, strategic planning is very difficult for us in that it requires two Decision Cycles—a Logistics Cycle to reallocate resources toward new programs and an Operational Cycle to implement that plan using the new infrastructure.

I suggest that *any* strategic program, be it ours or that of an adversary, requires two cycles to implement. A WMD program is a "program" long before any weapons of mass destruction actually exist. Every WMD program must go through a Logistics Cycle to build the weapons before it goes through an Operational Cycle to employ them. Surely to build a WMD program or to assemble a terrorist network is strategic and requires first building an infrastructure to build the WMD a nation might employ or the CBRNE (chemical, biological, radiological, nuclear or high-explosive) that terrorists might employ.

> LOGISTICS IS THE QUEEN OF BATTLES. The extent and variety of logistics preparations for modern war are reflected in the number of logistics and transportation items carried on indicator lists, which equal or exceed the number for any other topic. If we could be sure of

---

[35] Grabo, 17.
[36] Grabo, 18.

> knowing the extent, level and variety of logistics preparations at any time, we would not only have a very accurate grasp of the adversary's capabilities, we would probably also have very precise insight into his intent.[37]

The key to providing strategic warning on an adversary nation's WMD program or terrorist network's CBRNE program is to understand not only the Operations Decision Cycle but the Logistics Decision Cycle that precedes it. The logistics of research, development, production, and testing of WMD take years, sometimes decades, and can be exploited to provide strategic warning. Logistics for any terrorist operations are identical but smaller scale and dependent on a host nation.

Step 1 in building Warning Analysis for the Information Age is to build a methodology to model the target that accounts for his strategic planning and his need for a two-cycle planning process to build WMD or CBRNE.

Modeling How We Model—How Can We Provide Strategic Analysis to Build Our Own Strategic Plan?

> Having a computer is like having a clerk who can add one plus one, subtract one from one, and open a drawer and tell you if there is something in it. BUT he can do it VERY VERY fast.[38]

Once we have developed such a methodology, we need to develop ways to automate that method as much as possible. BUT, we need to remember that computers are tools that only do exactly what we program them to do. We must understand how we think and build strategic intelligence before we can automate it. I contend that efforts to date to "solve the database problem" have been flawed in that they are concerned with how to get data *into* the databases, not to get information *out*.

Step 2 in building Warning Analysis for the Information Age is to model how we think—build and test hypotheses—to provide strategic warning so that we can then develop tools to help automate the process.

---

[37] Grabo, 62.

[38] Dr. William Tolles, U.S Naval Postgraduate School, personal communication, 1971.

Modeling Ourselves—How Can We Reorient Our Intelligence Process to Empower the Warning Analyst to Think Strategically?

> "Network-centric warfare is not about technology. It is an emerging theory of war," said U.S. Navy Vice Adm. (ret.) Arthur K. Cebrowski, director of the Pentagon's force transformation office. "Power has shifted to the network," he said, and away from the Industrial-age view that power is derived from mass. Information, access to it and how fast it is delivered now determines combat power... "Net-centric warfare is not about the technology," an industry expert reaffirmed. "People would like to make it about technology, because it's easier to get their hands around it. This is about the network itself—different organizations and cultures—things that make operations difficult. It's about process—how to get people to share information, and how to change cultures.[39]

Once we have a methodology for strategic analysis and the computer tools to help automate it, we need to reorient our organizations to think cooperatively to provide strategic warning. Much has been said about the shift to "net-centric warfare" and how it can potentially revolutionize the way we fight. This concept is another way of verbalizing what we saw above: that in times of massive change a network is more effective than a hierarchy. But the current IC is based on Industrial-Age hierarchical models for information flow and leadership.

In the Industrial Age, organizations developed to get things done collectively using technology based on Newtonian models. The Newtonian paradigm concentrated on the operations part of the Decision Cycle (Decide and Act), and the current national infrastructure can *act efficiently* and almost *instantaneously* when decisions are made.

In the Information Age, organizations must be developed to make strategic plans aided by information technologies, but based on new models. The new paradigm must concentrate on the intelligence part of the Decisions Cycle (Observe and Orient), so that the future national infrastructure can *think effectively* and *cooperatively* to provide the plans for making those decisions.

Step 3 in building Warning Analysis for the Information Age is to "reorient the arrows" within the IC—both the information flow and leadership interactions—to

[39] William B. Scott and David Hughes, "Nascent Net-Centric War Gains Pentagon Toehold" *Aviation Week & Space Technology*, 27 Jan 2003, 50, 53.

provide mechanisms built on Information-Age thinking to be as close to a network as possible, when in the intelligence (Observe and Orient) part of our national Decision Cycle, to provide strategic intelligence and strategic warning.

Chapter 9

MODELING THE TARGET

How do we find out the adversary's strategic plan? Step 1 in building Warning Analysis for the Information Age is to build a methodology to model the target that accounts for his strategic planning and his need for a two decision-cycle planning process to build WMD or CBRNE.

Modeling WMD Networks—The Problem

If the final objective of warning analysis is the understanding of what the adversary is going to do, then the knowledge or recognition that he has decided to do something is the ultimate achievement... What should be of highest priority in the analytic process—the attempt to decide what the adversary has decided—is often shunted aside in favor of mere factual reporting of what is going on, which is obviously much easier and less controversial.[40]

[Multilayer Chart drawn by Michael Maskaleris]

> Human networks are distinct from electronic ones. They are not the Internet. They are political and emotional connections among people who must trust each other in order to function, like Colombian drug cartels and Basque separatists and the Irish Republican Army. Not to mention high-seas pirates, smugglers of illegal immigrants, and rogue brokers of weapons of mass destruction.[41]

WMD programs are networks built on multiple kinds of interactions: personal and organizational relationships, technical processes and flows, transportation and financial networks, and electronic connectivity networks. These interactions are often plotted as networks on a chart. Multilayer network diagrams very rapidly become unwieldy and incomprehensible because they contain information of multiple types which is plotted with no quantitative relationships among the nodes and distance or sequencing information in the links.

Visualizing Networks—the Dimensionality and Complexity Problems

Visualization: The Problem of High Dimensionality

- Humans can visualize very effectively in 2 dimensions; can identify patterns with difficulty in at most 5 or 6 dimensions

---

[40] Grabo, 103.

[41] Joel Garreau, "Disconnect the Dots," *Washington Post*, 17 Sep 2001, C1.

- Most low-dimensional projections of high-dimensional data are Gaussian, and therefore not very interesting
  Solution: find low-dimensional views or projections that are non-Gaussian.[42]

The world is 6-dimensional (6-D): 3 dimensions in space (x, y, z or Lat, Lon, and altitude), 1 dimension in time (t), and 2 dimensions in energy (enthalpy and entropy or H, S). Current network models do very well in spatial relationships, less well in temporal relationships, but very rarely consider energy relationships. Additionally, complex systems are composed of boxes-in-boxes and systems-of-systems, so that networks are also hierarchical. This adds a new problem of "drill-down," where an individual node at one level of complexity can be expanded to a network of its own by "looking inside" the node. Accordingly, a real-world network is really at least 18-dimensional, being 6-D at 3 levels of complexity (strategic, theater, and tactical). To plot an entire network one can, at best, hope to capture 2-D or 3-D "cross sections" that are meaningful and comprehensible and which are related in defined ways.

Visualizing and Understanding N-Dimensional Networks on 2-D Computer Screens

I suggest a series of axioms that will allow systematic construction of a nested series of network plots that account for the planning required to organize and build a WMD program or terrorist network. This formalization of dimensionality and complexity is designed to provide comprehensible ways to account for the interrelationships between the plots and to identify that a single event is multi-dimensional. Most importantly, these plots capture the planning and organization required for the overall program—and by showing the relationships of critical personalities they implicitly show doctrine.

Axiom: The key to understanding the operation of networks is "orienting the arrows" rather than "connecting the dots"

All biological systems are defined by what they *do*, not what they *are*. This includes military-political systems. The essence that defines them as biological

[42] Dean W. Abbott, Abbott Consulting, *Data Mining: Level II*, Class Handout, 2001. Cited hereafter as Abbott. Gaussian models are inherently Newtonian and suffer from all the limitations on Newtonian models described above.

systems is that they are organized to perform functions. Therefore, in biology the processes define the structures. By concentrating on the structures—be they missiles or buildings or CBW agents—and neglecting the processes they are used for, the intelligence community has lost a massive amount of very useful information contained in the reporting.

Processes inherently have a direction and, therefore, need to be plotted as arrows or vectors on a sequence chart (timeline) or as directed superior/subordinate relationships on an organization chart. Therefore, to understand how organizations can perform the processes required to build and employ WMD, we must orient the arrows rather than connect the dots.

> *Axiom: Plotting space, time, and energy requires maps, timelines, and organization charts.*

The laws of physics and chemistry indicate that the basic units of the universe are space, time, and energy. Therefore, visualization tools must reflect all three. The six units they represent (x, y, z, t, H, S) are independent variables and are therefore orthogonal or perpendicular. Accordingly, each represents an independent axis on any visualization plot.

- Maps define spatial relationships of entities. A plot of x vs. y, y vs. z, or z vs. x is a map. In the IC we usually use Latitude (Lat), Longitude (Lon), and altitude, and for most purposes altitude can be neglected. For most IC purposes, one of the "cross-sections" of the n-Dimensional (n-D) network will be a map with x and y axes of Lat and Lon.

- Timelines define temporal relationships or sequential events in the interactions of entities. A plot of "something" vs. t is a timeline. While actual time units may not be important for analysis in some cases, the time sequence of events is always important. For most IC purposes, the second "cross-section" of the n-D network will be a timeline with "something" on the vertical axis and time sequence—or series of events—plotted conventionally left to right.

- Organization charts define energy relationships among entities. The energy organization of ideal gases is conventionally visualized on a Maxwell-Boltzmann plot (see tonebox) which relates enthalpy and entropy. For biological and social organizations enthalpy corresponds to power and entropy corresponds to "degree of assembly" (see tonebox). For most IC purposes, the third required "cross-section" of the n-D network will be an organization chart with increas-

Defining Energy Relationships for Military-Political Organizations

Energy Plots for Chemists. Chemists define energy in terms of enthalpy and entropy. Enthalpy is a measure of bonds holding atoms together or of kinetic energy of moving molecules; entropy is a measure of the "disorder" of the system. For the simplest possible chemical system – the ideal gas – one can visualize the energy distribution of its molecules using the Maxwell-Boltzmann (M-B) plot. As shown, this plots the energy of any one molecule on the x axis versus the number of molecules having that energy on the y axis. Similar to the more recognizable "normal distribution" seen for visualization of grade distribution on a test, the M-B plot shows that there are a few gas molecules with very low energy or with very high energy and many with intermediate energies. Additionally, chemists define "activation energy" as an energy required for a molecule to undergo a chemical reaction, and on this plot only those molecules that are to the right of the "activation energy" line have enough energy to react.

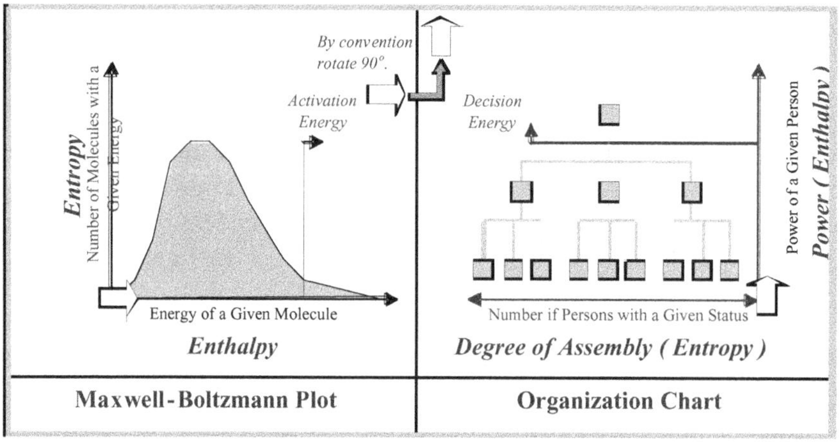

Energy Plots for Analysts. An organization chart is conceptually the same as a Maxwell-Boltzmann (M-B) plot – although by convention is rotated counter-clockwise ninety degrees from the M-B plot. In this case the vertical axis measures the relative power of a given person – much like the relative energy of a given molecule on the M-B plot. The horizontal axis represents "degree of assembly" in terms of the number of individuals (persons or organizational units) of an equivalent status or rank. There are implicit quantitative characteristics in an organization chart that can be defined explicitly by analogy with the chemical M-B plot:

- A "decision energy" (that corresponds to the chemist's activation energy) is defined on the vertical/power axis such that individuals above the line have the ability to make decisions that those below do not. For example, the person at the top can make decisions for the entire organization, while mid-level persons can make decisions for only their individual units. In chemistry, enthalpy is a measure of the ability of an individual to make or break chemical bonds; in analysis, power is a measure of the ability of an individual to make decisions and have them carried out.
- The number of individuals at any given level on the vertical/power axis represents the complexity of the organization and the difficulty in assembling and maintaining the organizational structure. For example, an organization with only two mid-level managers will be able to perform fewer different kinds of tasks than one with ten mid-level managers but will have an easier time in coordinating those tasks. In chemistry, entropy is a measure of the number of possible ways a system can be arranged; in analysis, entropy or "degree of assembly" is a measure of the number of possible interactions required to perform a task.

ing "power" plotted vertically and "degree of assembly" plotted horizontally.

Neglecting the third spatial dimension (altitude), 6-D networks can be plotted at a single level of complexity with a single set of three plots: a map, a timeline, and an organization chart.

Axiom: Biological and military-political systems can be modeled as a series of nested Decision Cycles (OODA Cycles)

Biological systems are defined by what they *do* rather than what they are. As introduced above biology texts define "life" as the ability to: (1) extract and store energy from the environment; (2) sense and respond to the environment; (3) reproduce; and (4) evolve. Col John Boyd defined military units by a "decision cycle," or "OODA Cycle," where they: **O**bserve, **O**rient, **D**ecide, and **A**ct. He defines the military unit by what it *does*, which is totally consistent with the process definition of life. Also, note that each of the abilities in the biologist's definition of life is individually an OODA cycle. Thus a basic visualization of any biological or military-political system is a timeline.

In each of these nested OODA Cycles there is a plan—a systematic series of steps from conception (of what needs to be done) through maturity (of actually getting it done).

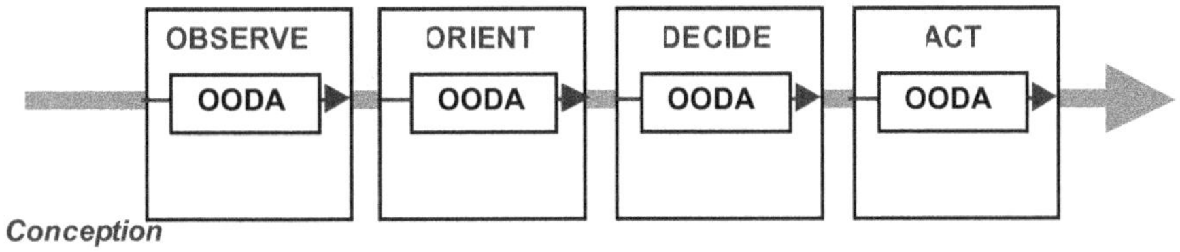

One can capture the decisionmaking of a biological organism or military-political organization by a timeline that captures the nested Decision Cycles from conception to maturity.

Axiom: The steps from planning to completion of a task can be visualized on a timeline with "degree of assembly" plotted against the time sequence of the steps in assembly.

The Second Law of Thermodynamics states that the entropy of the universe is always increasing; that is, the world as a whole is always disassembling or falling apart. For example, if one takes a glass full of water and drops it on the floor it will "disassemble" rather dramatically as it shatters and the pieces fly everywhere. But it is highly unlikely that those pieces would, on their own, assemble and fly back into your hand. Thus, if one plotted the "degree of assembly" of the world versus time, one would see an increasing number of possible states over the timeline. Biological systems appear to "beat" the Second Law by extracting and using energy and matter from the environment to build new components or systems. Similarly, WMD programs collect energy and materials to assemble and use those weapons. Therefore, one can visualize a WMD program by tracking the assembly of the weapon.

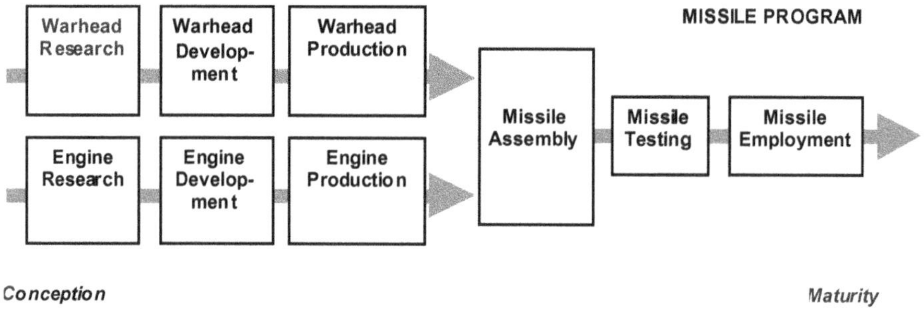

In the Program Timeline:

- Time in terms of sequence of steps is plotted left to right.
- Each step in the program is plotted as a component process in the overall plan. Note that each step is implicitly an OODA cycle.
- The vertical axis is "degree of assembly" where the objects at each time step represent the number of objects being manipulated in that part of the program. Note that many different research projects are often required for a few development projects in one overall program and that "degree of assembly" increases to the right.
- Each program step can be subdivided into its own component program steps.
- The program timeline follows the program from conception to maturity and includes the planning and Research and Development (R&D) phases as well. This means that the object of the program may not exist for most of the program; for example, in a SCUD missile program, a SCUD missile does not exist until the "missile assembly" step.

> *Axiom: In a Program Timeline each program step can be expanded to include the input materials, energy, and personnel required for its completion.*

Biological systems extract energy and materials from the environment and use them to build new components or systems. Tracking the inputs into any process step on the Program Timeline is important because:

- The status of the entire process as well as the characteristics of the process can often be deduced through knowledge of the inputs. For example, much can be known about a missile warhead factory by knowing: how much electrical power it consumes, whether or not uranium or plutonium is among the raw materials, the qualifications of its engineers, or the types of equipment ordered and when they were ordered.
- Knowing the location of the process allows linking the Timeline with the Map.
- Knowing the personnel and their organizations allows linking the Timeline with the Organization Chart.

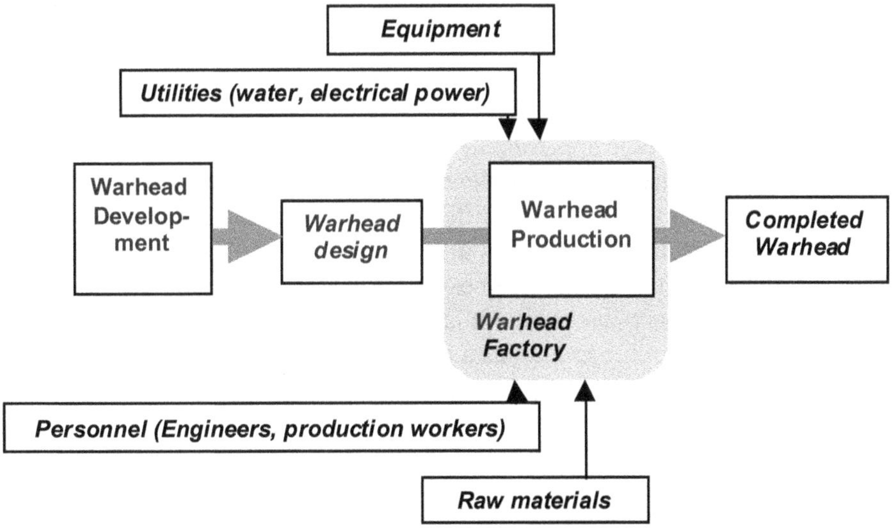

Axiom: Each visualization plot requires a "drill-down" capability to reflect the hierarchical nature of biological and military-political organizations.

All non-routine or unusual actions emanating from the national level result from some kind of decisions. They don't just happen. This is true of both military and political actions. When something unusual occurs, particularly something that increases the adversary's capability to take military action or is otherwise potentially ominous, the

> analyst should ask such questions as: What does this suggest of the adversary's plans? What prompted him to do this? What kind of decision has been taken which would account for this action?[43]

Biological systems require an infrastructure to accomplish the Decision Cycles required to extract energy from the environment, sense and respond to the environment, reproduce, and evolve. Military-political systems have the same requirements since they are biological systems. The nested nature of the Decision Cycles that describe such systems will also be reflected in hierarchical nested maps, timelines, and organization charts needed to describe them. For example, the timeline for warhead production above could be further subdivided to indicate how the design, utilities, equipment, and raw materials come together to build a warhead. Similarly, the Organization Chart for the production factory is nested inside an organization chart for the military-industrial complex and could be subdivided into departments and divisions and even individual leaders, engineers, or workers.

Axiom: Program Timelines and Organization Charts represent orthogonal visualizations.

> Another simplistic approach to the decisionmaking question, which also occurs surprisingly frequently, is to assume that political and military decisions are taken by different groups and are somehow not related to each other... This is highly erroneous, at least in countries where the national leadership exerts effective command and control over the military forces, and it is particularly erroneous where the political leadership maintains a monopoly on the decisionmaking process and the military undertakes virtually nothing on its own.[44]

[43] Grabo, 104-105

[44] Grabo, 107.

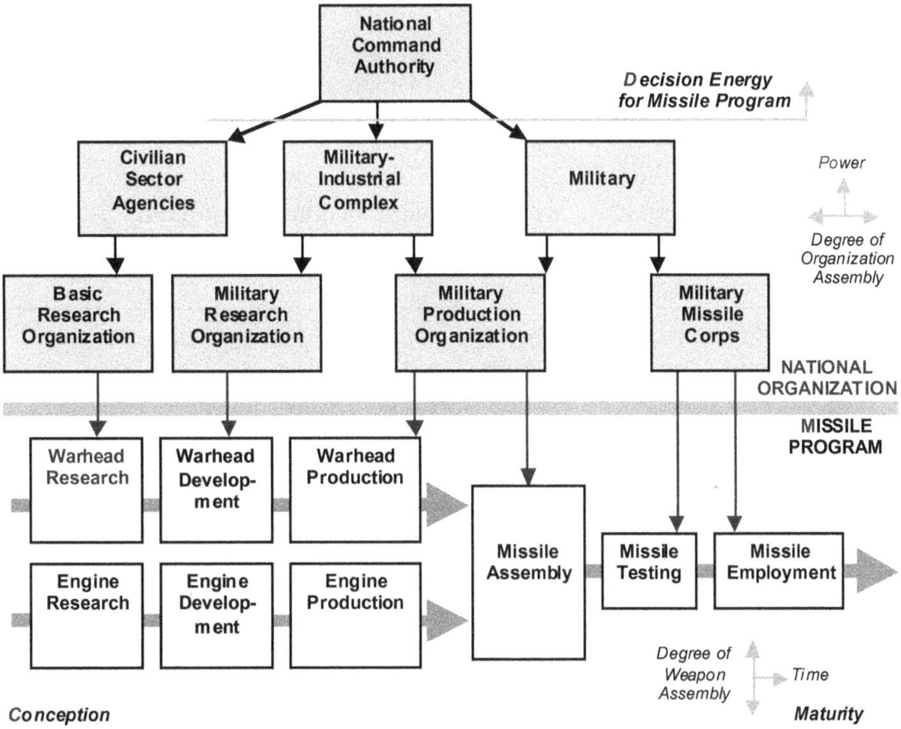

Program timelines indicate a "degree of assembly" of the weapon in a WMD program while organization charts indicate a "degree of assembly" of people into organizations. These are directly related in that organizations are organized to accomplish specific goals. For example, for a missile program the two plots overlay as shown above.

The Program Timeline and Organization Chart are related in that:

- The individual steps in the Program Timeline require a specific organization to plan and accomplish them.
- The individual organizations on the Organization Chart are arranged to reflect the planning and coordination necessary to accomplish the specific tasks.
- Overall coordination of any program requires coordination of the organizations needed to accomplish its goals; therefore, any program will require a person who is the overall leader/coordinator for that pro-

gram. That person's status will be above the "decision energy" required for the task.

In analysis of any program, the Program Timeline and Organization Chart provide complementary (orthogonal) visualizations:

- The Organization Chart indicates the personal and organizational interactions required for planning and executing the program.
- The Program Timeline indicates the actual sequence of events in accomplishment of the program.

> *Axiom: Organization Charts, Program Timelines, and National Maps must be used in an integrated manner to track the organization and operation of networks.*

> Additionally, there are two general guidelines that will assist the analyst in perceiving the enemy's most likely course of action through a fog of deception:
>
> *Separate the wheat from the chaff.* Weed out from the mass of incoming material all information of doubtful reliability or origin and assemble that information which is either known to be true (the "facts") or which has come from reliable sources which have no personal axes to grind or reasons to deceive...
>
> *Keep your eyes on the hardware.* In the end, the adversary must launch operations with his military forces and what they do will be the ultimate determinant of his intent.[45]

The objects and processes required for the operation of a network exist in a 6-D world. Biological systems and organizations are different from physical systems in that they control energy for tasks and programs that require both planning and coordination to accomplish, and a network of interacting parts is required for this. Thus, visualization of biological and military-political networks requires a concerted effort to capture this.

Enthalpy is a measure of the power stored in chemical bonds. Thus, building requires marshaling energy, and WMD programs are basically building programs. Therefore:

- Timelines must reflect the "building" that goes on in the program by:
    - ❑ Identifying the energy and materials required to build the components at each step of the program.

[45] Grabo, 131.

- ❑ Identifying and tracking the final product of the program—the weapon. (This is customarily done using maps.)

- ■ Organization charts must reflect how an organization accomplishes "building" by:
  - ❑ Identifying and tracking the person with the "decision energy" required to coordinate each step in the process.
  - ❑ Remembering that organizations work from a plan. The organizational infrastructure and the timeline will be consistent with that plan.

Entropy is a measure of "degree of assembly." Biological systems apparently defy the Second Law of Thermodynamics in that they organize and assemble rather than disorganize and disassemble. Therefore:

- ■ Timelines must reflect assembly over time as the program matures.
- ■ Organization Charts must reflect the assembly of people into the functional teams required for the assembly steps in the program

Axiom: Analysis must integrate top-down and bottom-up modeling.

Complex systems are hierarchical in that they can be described as a series of nested boxes-in-boxes or systems-of-systems. Every system can be described as an individual with system parameters to describe its behavior or as a unit composed of smaller systems operating cooperatively.

Emergent Properties—Characteristics of Individuals not Units

When viewed as a unit, the system is united but unitary; that is, it can be described as *e pluribus unum*, "one made of many."

When viewed as an individual, the system is indivisible; it cannot be broken down into smaller pieces without losing it identity. The concept of "half-a-fruit-fly" or "half-a-carbon-atom" or "half a missile assembly plant" is meaningless.

Emergent properties are those which apply to the system as an individual. Smaller systems comprise the unit, but it is only when they are truly unitary and can be treated as an individual that a new emergent property can be defined. For example, the property of life "emerges" at the cellular level; even though the cell is composed of a defined structure of macromolecules, DNA and proteins cannot be described as alive, only a cell can. Similarly, evolution "emerges" at the species level; even though species are composed of populations of individual organisms, organisms individually cannot evolve, only species can. Accordingly, there are characteristics of a "baseball team," or a "Marine Corps company," or a "missile assembly plant" that can apply only as long as the unit can continue to function as an individual entity.

Thus when describing a system, an emergent property can only be applied at a given level of complexity thus requiring that the system be described as an individual. Theoretically, one could also describe the system as a unit and by applying an appropriate non-linear model describe the cooperative interactions of the smaller individuals that provide for the emergent property. In practice it is usually only feasible to model the system as a unit (an integrated system comprising individuals) to understand why the property emerges, then measure that property by describing the system as an individual. For example, one could model a warship using the individual components—turbines, pumps, compressors—and calculate its top speed, turning radius, and other tactical characteristics. But in practice, it is much more straightforward to take the approach of *Jane's Fighting Ships* and tabulate the top speed and tactical characteristics and use the table to describe the ships as individuals.

There are two basic kinds of methodologies to model the world:

- Bottom-up models describe systems as units composed of smaller subsystems. One catalogs all the different kinds of subsystems and describes their interactions, then uses the characteristics of those interactions to describe the behavior of the system.
- Top-down models describe systems as individuals that are indivisible. One measures the behavior of the system as a whole in multiple experiments, then tabulates the properties that describe the system. Once the system function is described it can be subdivided into component systems performing component processes.

Bottom-Up Models

See networks as objects connected by lines.

“Connect the dots.”

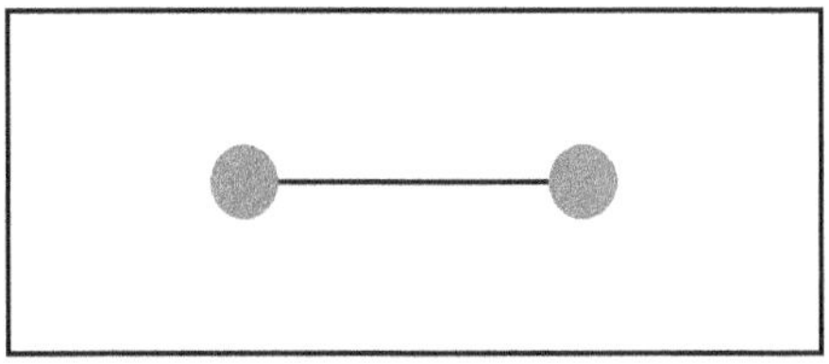

The process of model-building begins with two objects that interact.

One builds a bottom-up model by adding new objects that interact with those objects.

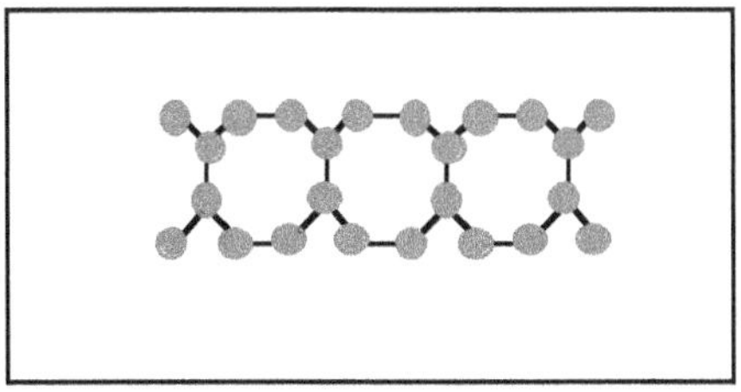

One continues to assemble objects until the unit is complete (and implicitly is functional).

Top-Down Models

See networks as arrows connected by objects.

Orient the arrows.”

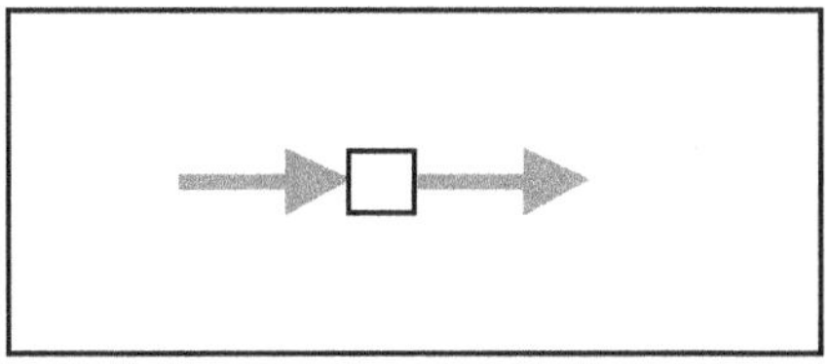

The process of model-building begins with a single object that reacts to an input process to perform an output process.

One builds a top-down model by burrowing within the object to break down the initial process into smaller processes.

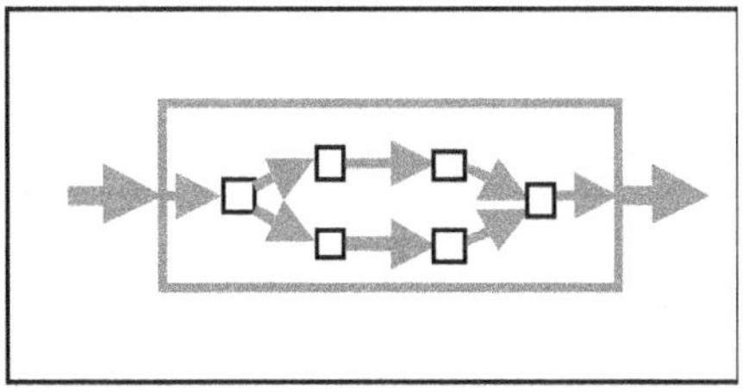

One continues to subdivide processes until the process cannot be subdivided further or the objects are indivisible.

We are more familiar with Bottom-Up models not only because most collection is done on given types of objects but also because the way we reason—using English syntax is also inherently Bottom-Up.

Bottom-Up Models

Nouns separated by verbs.

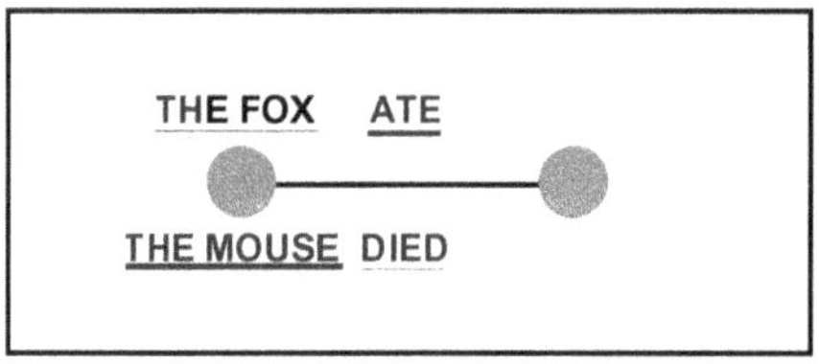

A syntax where objects act on other objects.

Top-Down Models

Verbs separated by nouns.

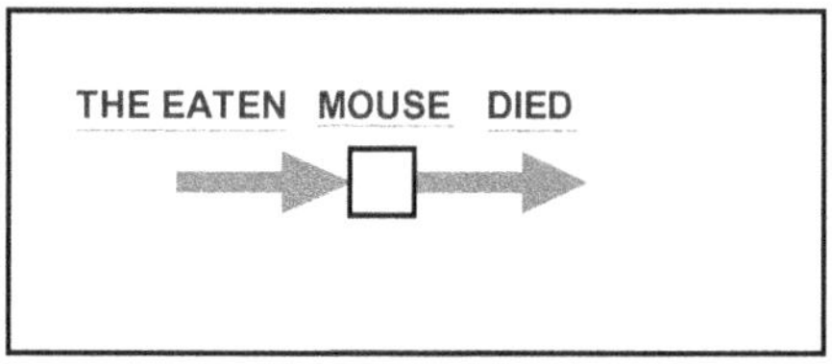

A syntax of cause and effect—an input process causes an output process.

Most models are Bottom-Up models where we observe the individual objects that must be assembled to form a unit. There are only a few models we use often that are Top-Down models.

For example:

Bottom-Up Models

X-ray crystallography.

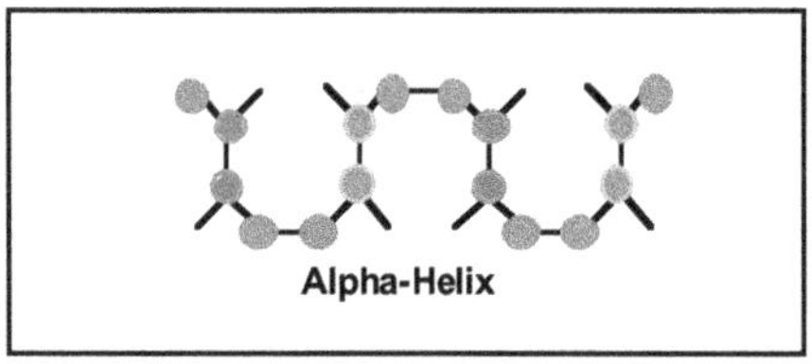

Experimental data are used to model structure.

Can demonstrate structure directly, but can only infer function.

X-ray crystallography can show directly what an enzyme's active site *is*, but not what is *does*.

Top-Down Models

Michaelis-Menten Enzyme Kinetics

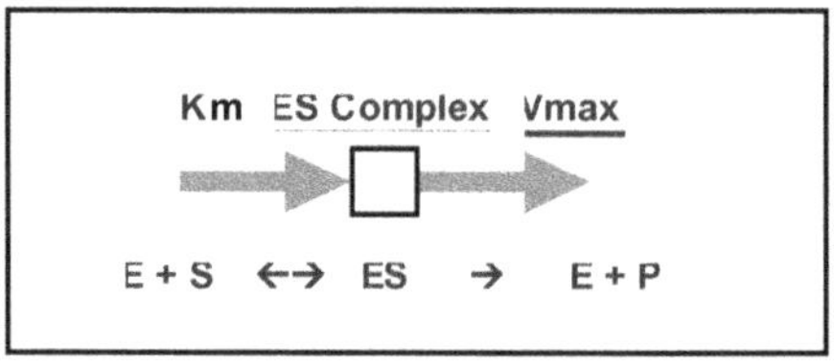

Experimental data are used to model function.

Can demonstrate function directly, but can only infer structure.

Enzyme kinetics can show directly what an enzyme's active site *does*, but not what it *is*.

The two kinds of models are complementary but mutually exclusive. In a single type of experiment you can build only one kind of model. If you design a Bottom-Up experiment, you can determine structure and then use the characteristics of that structure to deduce what that structure does. If you design a Top-Down experiment, you can determine function and then use the characteristics of that function to deduce what the structure must be.

For Bottom-Up thinking—Structure determines Function.
For Top-Down thinking—Function determines Structure.

To fully characterize a system's structure and function you must perform at least two experiments—at least one bottom-up and one top-down.

For the intelligence process, there are advantages and disadvantages to each kind of model:

- A top-down model provides a notional network. This is good for collection planning but provides no hard intelligence by itself.
- A bottom-up model provides a real-world network. This provides hard intelligence but is consistent with haphazard collection planning.
- A top-down model tells you where to look and what to look for but cannot provide intelligence until you actually look.
- A bottom-up model keeps track of what you've found but cannot provide guidance on where to look next.

What is needed is an integrated approach that combines top-down and bottom-up modeling. Using a top-down model of nested processes on a timeline or nested organizations on an organization chart, one can begin to fill in the hard intelligence by function on the timeline or by association on the organization chart. This sorts the "puzzle pieces" by type. The pieces of hard intelligence can then be assembled bottom-up in each category. This kind of integrated approach can be used to build real-world networks and is both good for collection planning and for assembling hard intelligence into a coherent picture.

Multidimensional Analysis—Visualizing WMD Networks in 6-D

> Kathleen Carley, director of the Center for Computational Analysis of Social and Organizational Systems at Carnegie Mellon University, says: "One of the things that leads to the ability to adapt is who knows who and who knows what. The higher that is, the better the group's flexibility. But you can reduce the number of times the group can communicate or congregate."[46]

[46] Joel Garreau, "Disconnect the Dots," *Washington Post*, 17 Sep 2001, C1, C2.

The integrated method described above, which will be termed "Multidimensional Analysis" (MDA), combines top-down and bottom-up models and represents those models in 6-D using maps, timelines, and organization charts. Such an approach has been applied to strategic analysis of the North Korean BW program, Russian biotechnology program, and the Al Qaeda CBRNE program. Results of those analyses are presented as classified case studies, and lessons learned from those studies indicate the good prospects for a straightforward application of Multidimensional Analysis to WMD and CBRNE programs.

The lessons learned reiterate the non-Newtonian quantum assumptions for strategic modeling of biological and organizational systems: History matters, and people make decisions, so you need to follow the people to learn intent.

The methodology is based on knowing where to look and what to look for in detail based on top-down modeling and also knowing how to build a 6-D model by directed bottom-up assembly of the collected data. What do we look for? Where do we look for it? How do we assemble it into a multidimensional model?

Strategic Analysis of a WMD program—What Do We Look For?

Multidimensional analysis assumes that a WMD program is built by people and that they interact within organizations as they gather and assemble supplies and equipment to build WMD. Therefore, we need to look for interactions of several types of entities—people, places, things, and organizations—in space, time, and energy (both power and organization). Therefore, whether we think bottom-up and connect the dots or top-down and orient the arrows, the model will be built of nested entities and the processes they perform.

A simple way to relate the 6-D approach to more familiar modeling methods is to think of the questions one asks when writing a complete story: Who? What? When? Where? Why? and How? *Maps* tell us **where** the program is and **how** the entities move to assemble the WMD. *Timelines* tell us **what** is needed to assemble the WMD and **when** those assembly steps occurred (or likely will occur). *Organization charts* tell us who is building the WMD and—through analysis of how they are organized—**why** they are doing things in a particular way.

The Maps, Timelines, and Organization Charts we will draw for a WMD or CBRNE program show all the component entities and processes performed by those entities to assemble the WMD. Each plot is built of nodes and links between those nodes, but note that on Maps and Organization Charts the nodes are entities and the links are processes but on Timelines the nodes are processes and the links are entities. Once the data are plotted in those formats, we can draw actionable intelligence by straightforward analysis of the individual plots.

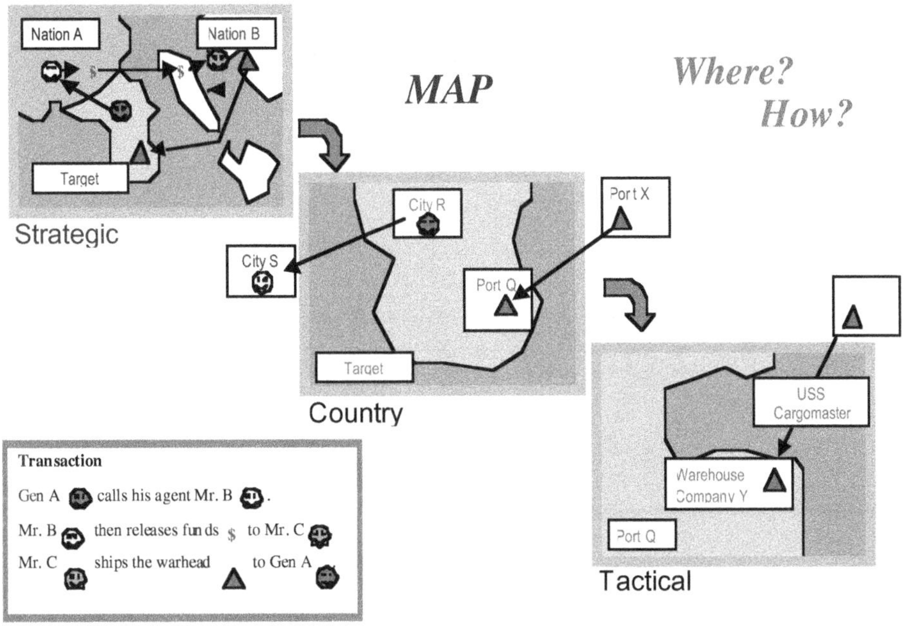

MAPS: Where? How?

Nodes = geographical entities — facilities and the position of those facilities.

Links = transportation processes — transportation routes. Here we usually define the routes by the entities that do the transporting, e.g., trucks, aircraft, or ships, and the terminal facilities for that transportation, e.g. facilities, airports, ports.

Maps identify interdiction points — Entity = facility to target; Link = route to interdict.

TIMELINE What? When?

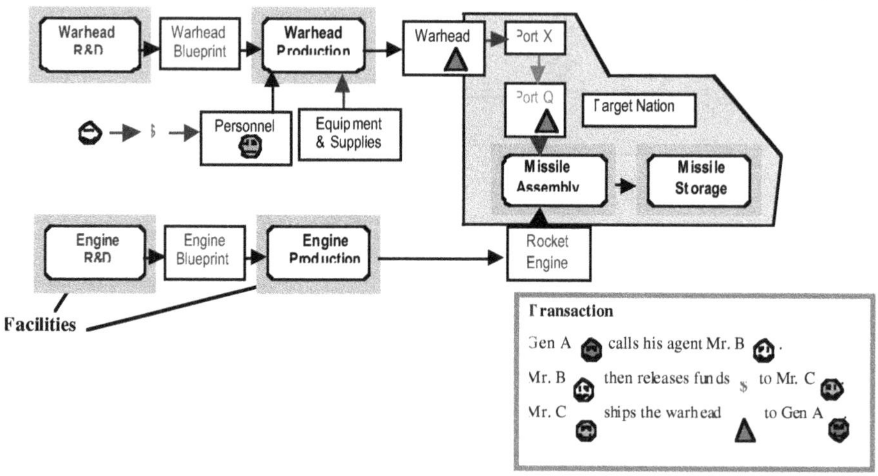

TIMELINES: What? When?

Nodes = critical processes in WMD fabrication — research, development, production, testing, and employment of both the payload and the delivery device.

Links = component entities in WMD fabrication — research provides protocols for development, development provides blueprints for production, production provides the payload or delivery device to the assembly plant, and the assembly plant provides the completed munitions to the forces in the field.

Timelines identify progress toward fielding a WMD system. If we know the most complete component produced to date, we can estimate progress toward weaponization. By identifying the total number of additional processes toward weaponization, we can estimate the time needed to field a WMD.

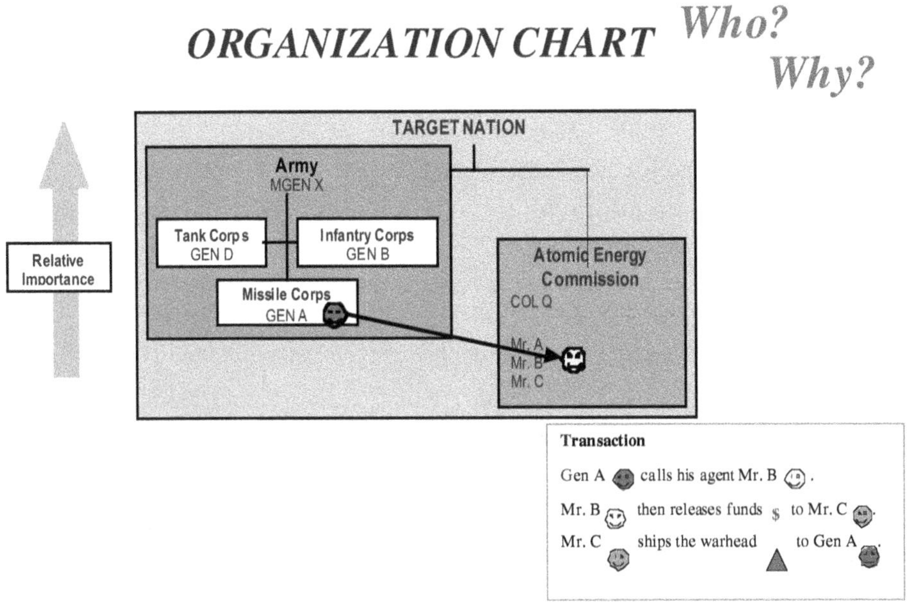

ORGANIZATION CHARTS: Who? Why?

Nodes = critical organizations in WMD program

Links = tasking or funding or information exchange

Organization Charts identify interrelationships of the organizations and people in the program. The node that is highest in organization is the one in charge. The node with most links is critical for procurement, funding, or operations.

The key to multidimensional analysis is in building both bottom-up structural models and top-down process models for all the entities. A photograph or x-ray or CAT scan of a person is a structural model and tells you who or what the person is. However, a résumé, which is a process model of the same person, is much more valuable in assessing a person's plans and intentions because it tells you what a person can do.

The core of multidimensional analysis is to combine the conventional structural models with process models, résumés if you wish. For a person that would obviously be a résumé (or a scientific résumé—a curriculum vitae or CV). For an organization that would be an organizational history. For a place or thing, such as a facility or factory, or nuclear warhead or missile, that would be a project history.

We need to keep in mind that a WMD program will exist long before the weapon itself actually exists and that the project history begins with the decision to begin research on the feasibility of building the weapon.

> *FOLLOW THE PEOPLE... **They will lead you to the projects.***
>
> - Smart people are needed to build WMD.
> - Informal networks (Party, family, teachers) can be more important than traditional chain-of-command.
> - Scientists and Engineers are specialists. A WMD program requires an appropriate mix of expertise.
> - Scientists gain prestige by publications and presentations.

Building a Curriculum Vitae or Technical Résumé

With the goal of building as complete a résumé as possible on the key personnel within the WMD program, we can exploit many kinds of source material. Examples here are directed toward analysis of a state-run BW program although similar reasoning can be applied to state-run chemical weapons, nuclear, or missile programs.

- Department Rosters — These can sometimes indicate links to military programs.
- Company Brochures — These may also indicate links to military.
- Résumés — Sometimes these can be obtained directly.
- Curricula Vitae (CVs) — Academic scientist résumés are often posted online.
- Business cards (can provide addresses, phone numbers, E-mail).
- Catalogs
- Publications

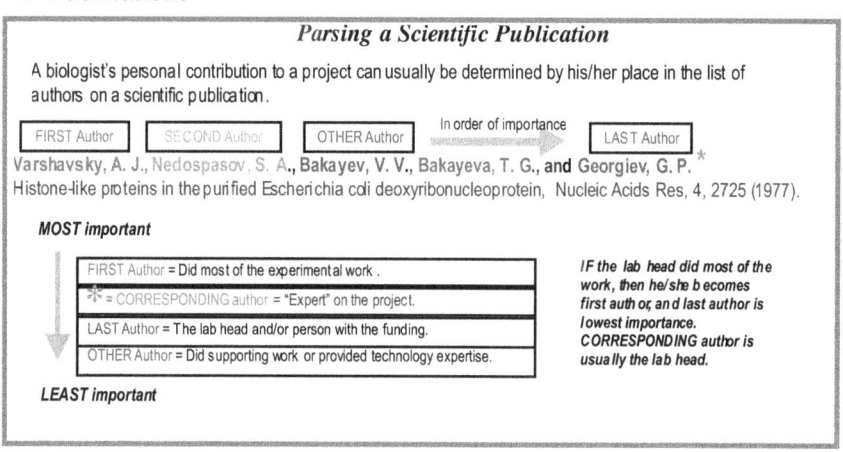

Parsing a Scientific Publication

A biologist's personal contribution to a project can usually be determined by his/her place in the list of authors on a scientific publication.

FIRST Author | SECOND Author | OTHER Author | In order of importance → | LAST Author *

Varshavsky, A. J., Nedospasov, S. A., Bakayev, V. V., Bakayeva, T. G., and Georgiev, G. P. *
Histone-like proteins in the purified Escherichia coli deoxyribonucleoprotein, Nucleic Acids Res, 4, 2725 (1977).

MOST important

FIRST Author = Did most of the experimental work.
* = CORRESPONDING author = "Expert" on the project.
LAST Author = The lab head and/or person with the funding.
OTHER Author = Did supporting work or provided technology expertise.

LEAST important

IF the lab head did most of the work, then he/she becomes first author, and last author is lowest importance. CORRESPONDING author is usually the lab head.

Med.line *(med'lin)* ***vt.*** *–lined, -lining. (slang term used by US biologists). to reconstruct a curriculum vitae or résumé for a biologist using the online PubMed web site from the National Institute of Health (NIH).*

The entire career of a biologist can often be reconstructed by tracing all his or her publications online on Pubmed and following: projects worked on, institutional affiliations including years of first and last pubs at an institution, and coauthors.

Scientist résumés or CVs can be pieced together by analysis of their publications, conference presentations and interviews of sources about their career. Scientists can be suspicious when collaborating on BW, CW or nuclear dual-use projects and/ or when linked to military programs.

- Construct CVs by "Medlining"
- Expertise — What do they know?
- Links — Where did they learn it?
- Who do they know?
- Publication record
- Did they disappear from the literature?
- What did they publish when they re-emerged?

A prolonged lack of publications (especially when later publications are state-of-the-art) can indicate that a scientist has worked on classified projects.

Tracking a Biologist's Career by Publications

Biologists' careers can be tracked by their publication records.

- A *PhD student* will usually publish for 3 to 8 years with his/her mentor or advisor as last author.

- A *Postdoctoral Fellow* will also usually include his/her advisor as senior (last) author.

- A *Bench Scientist* will usually have FIRST/SECOND author publications with advisor LAST for PhD and Postdoc then move to primarily LAST author papers when establishing his/her own lab.

- A "*Gene Jockey*" (Biotechnologist) will usually have FIRST/SECOND author publications with advisor LAST for PhD and Postdoc. Afterwards he/she will have many OTHER author publications with many different LAST (senior) authors indicating that he/she is providing biotechnology expertise on many different projects.

- A Biologist with many OTHER author publications with the same LAST (senior) author is usually a bench scientist working as a senior research scientist in the lab of that senior biologist.

- A talented biologist will have FIRST or SECOND author publications when a PhD student and Postdoc. Scientists with mostly OTHER publications either don't last or end up doing bench work for someone else throughout their careers.

Building an Institutional Profile

Any WMD program depends on R&D and production facilities, both for the BW, CW, or nuclear payload and the delivery system. One can track the process that occurs inside a technical facility by following the inputs and outputs to that facility. Again a BW facility will be profiled as an example.

Facilities associated with BW or involved in dual-use biological R&D can be identified by the biologists they employ and the biotechnology equipment they acquire. Biotechnology projects usually require three different kinds of biological expertise: classical biologists who are experts on the microorganism, biotechnologists who are bioengineering experts, and production specialists who are experts on growing large-scale amounts of microorganisms. The biotechnology expertise and biotech equipment can be significant when linked to projects on microorganisms that can be used as BW agents or bioengineered into BW agents. Note that the "Babool Microbiology Institute in Karjakistan" can refer to either an organization or facility—or both—dependent on the context.

Biotechnology equipment used in BW or dual-use projects includes:

- Genetic Engineering R&D
- DNA Synthesizers
- PCR (Polymerase Chain Reaction)
  Thermal Cyclers
  Taq (Thermus Aquaticus) DNA Polymerase
- Large-Scale Production/Processing Of Microorganisms
- Fermenters
- Bioreactors
- Freeze-Dryers

Assessing whether a facility or institution is dual-use or actually involved in a BW program can be problematic. There are clues to determine if a facility is merely biomedical or biological R&D or dual-use or BW-associated:

- DUAL-USE FACILITIES
  Declared under Biological Warfare Convention (BWC)
  Brochures, catalogs, products can point to dual-use projects
  Biohazard Containment for infectious microorganisms
    BL-4 (maximum containment) or BL-3 facilities
    Special air handling systems
- BW FACILITIES are usually associated with the military
    Special security measures, bunkers, underground sites
    Military chain of command, telephone books

Tracking a BW or Dual-Use Biotechnology Program
A Top-Down Process Model

A Facility involved in a BW or dual-use biomedical program can be characterized by projects, scientists, and equipment and supplies.

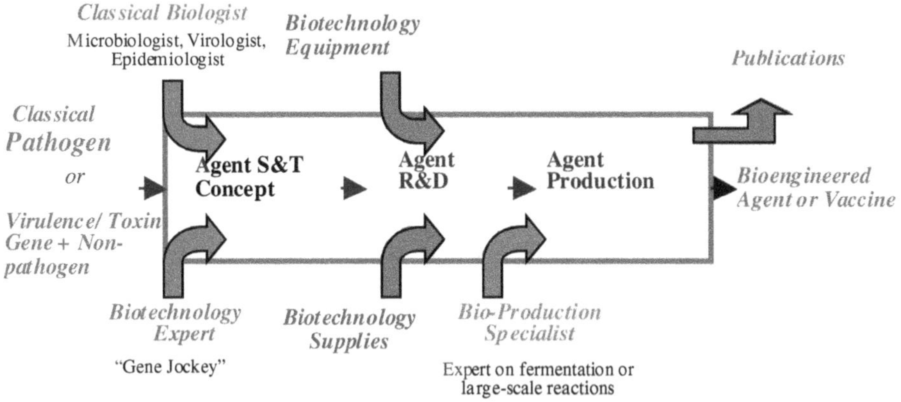

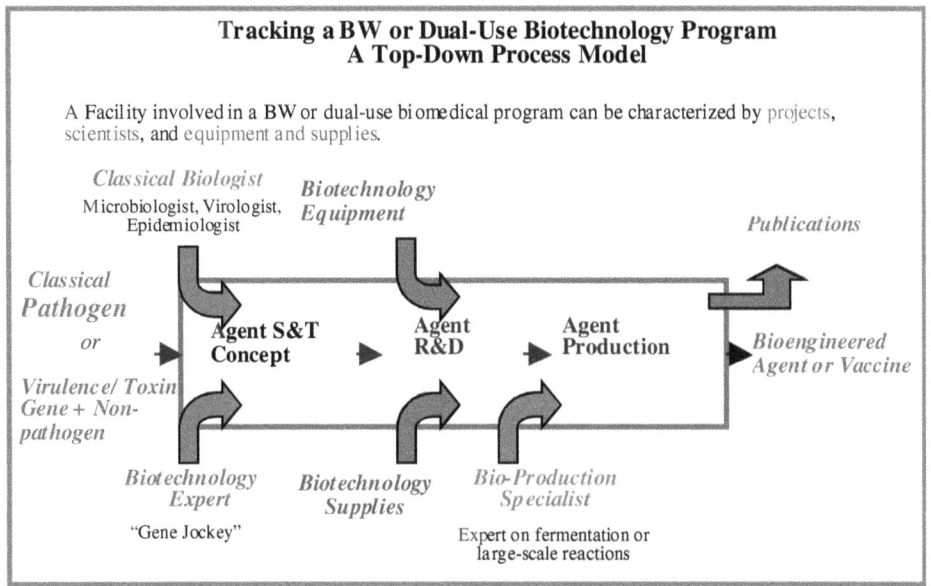

Strategic Analysis of a WMD Program: Where Do We Look for Data?

Multidimensional Analysis is aimed at integrating top-down models of WMD programs to provide the framework for the kinds of data that need to be collected, and bottom-up models that take reporting and build assessments.

The top-down model provides a convenient tool for sorting data and looking for more related data. For example, if a report indicates that the "Babool Microbiology Institute of Karjakistan" is involved in BW research, the analyst can begin to ask a series of questions:

- *Who* works at the Institute? Who do Institute workers visit and talk to? Which agency runs the Institute? Which agency is the parent agency subordinate to?
- *What* projects are going on at the Institute? What equipment and supplies do they order? What kinds of technical resources and lab containment are required to support those projects?
- *Where* is the Institute located? Where are the component structures of the facility? Where do the supplies and equipment come from?
- *When* was the Institute formed? When was the facility built? When were people hired? When were the projects started?
- *Why*? (The toughest question...which will be addressed later).
- *How* are supplies brought into the facility? How are products taken from the facility?

Answers to these specific types of questions lead to asking new questions of the same kinds. If we find out that Dr. Boris Borisovich works for the Microbiology Institute, we can proceed as above, asking the same kinds of questions about him as an individual. The same applies if we find out that the Microbiology Institute is housed in two buildings, one in downtown Babool and one inside a fenced area in the nearby army base or if we learn that the Microbiology Institute is subordinate to the Karjakistan Ministry of Health. We aim to collect data to construct resumes for all key *persons*, histories for all nested *organizations*, descriptions and histories of all related facilities (*places*), and histories of all projects (*things*).

Multidimensional Analysis is built on the assumptions that context is very important for navigating. If I can build a detailed "maps" in 6-D, and place an entity on those maps, I can deduce where it came from and where it's going. History matters.

By applying Multidimensional Analysis (MDA) methods to several projects (see Case Studies), in the author's experience there were several unexpected lessons learned about how the different intelligence collection methods—"INTs"—support MDA and how MDA can in turn support the individual INTs in return.

Human Intelligence (HUMINT) reporting is by far the most important data source for MDA. All the questions of who, what, when, where, why, and how can be asked to any HUMINT source, but we have found that many of the required data bits have already been collected but remain in the databases because they were either not valued or considered "too hard" to search for and use. In addition, the kinds of questions asked through MDA also tend to mitigate the major problem in WMD analysis of finding technically competent sources.

For example, a janitor from the Babool Microbiology Institute has defected. By previous standards he would be discounted as a source because the most critical BW-related questions such as "What kinds of microorganisms do they grow?" would obviously be well beyond his expertise. But for MDA there are many questions for which he could provide very valuable and reliable answers. Who is the Director of the Institute? Who is your superior, and who does he work for? Have any Party dignitaries or military officers visited the Institute? Who did they meet? Which labs did they visit? Whose name is on the door to those labs? When you collect trash, are there any rooms off-limits for collection? Is there any special handling you do of any trash or is any put in special kinds of plastic bags or sealed containers? Are there any animal or plant facilities that need to be cleaned? By thinking of building WMD as a process mediated by people and organizations, a multitude of questions can be asked that a janitor—or almost any kind of source—can answer.

The redundancy of the detailed kinds of information collected in support of MDA also provides an excellent reliability check; both on the data and on the sources. In the example plots in the Figures above, General A ordered a warhead through his intermediary Mr. B. That transaction could be validated from a variety of sources:

- Phone intercepts could provide names and items of discussion.
- Recovery of phone numbers from either General A's or Mr. B's phonebook could indicate a link.
- Information from a variety of sources that General A was the Director of the Missile Corp and Mr. B. was associated with the Atomic Energy Commission would provide additional context.
- The location of both their offices as well as the area code for their phones would cross-correlate to provide information on their organizations and facilities.
- Another phone conversation between Mr. B. and Mr. C would have been followed by an invoice sent or faxed, a transfer of money, a receipt for the money, a receipt for the delivered item, and finally a round on interactions confirming completion of the order. Intercept of any one of those, in the appropriate time frame, would validate any of the other data.

Note that the reporting at this level soon begins to cross-validate source reliability. If the janitor in General A's building came forward, one could check pieces of the story against his recollections of what office the General worked in during what time period and if he was even in the country at the appropriate time. In short, MDA aims to collect data at multiple levels of granularity which will ultimately cross-validate and also, as a spin-off, usually can encounter something that any source with access—with any kind of expertise—can provide reliably. For an MDA analyst, having access to the supply clerk (like Radar O'Reilly in the MASH TV show) may as valuable as having access to the General.

MDA also can overcome the usual reaction that it's "too hard" to track individual people. A report on a North Korean microbiologist named Kim Chong-Ho is, at first glance, impossible to track any further since querying for "Kim" or "Kim Chong" or "Dr. Kim" in a database will return thousands of hits—mostly extraneous. This is compounded by the translation problem in that his name could also be reported as "Kim Jong-Ho" or even "Kim Jong-O." In MDA, the analyst would likely note that name when first encountered, and wait for another link to make tracking easier. For example, if Dr. Kim was linked to the "Yang-Ho Anthrax Institute," all the reporting available on that institute could be rechecked for any references to a "Dr. Kim." As more cross-correlations become available, re-searching databases for the correct person becomes easier, even though it still means having to read through irrelevant articles to separate "Dr. Kim Chong-Ho, the microbiologist from the Yang-Ho Anthrax Institute" from "Dr. Kim Chong-O, the Army Colonel from the Yang-Ho Army Base." The same reasoning goes for separating or correlating institutions that have multiple possible name translations such as the "Microbiology Institute" vs "Germ Research Center" vs "Microbiological Research Academy."

HUMINT-directed HUMINT targeting is aided by using MDA because the top-down approach provides a framework for asking relevant questions. By knowing not only where a source is from but also when he was there and who he was in the organizational structure, questions can be worded to confirm what is already known about his location in the 6-D model for the program with which he is associated. For example, if a source came from the "Yang-Ho Anthrax Institute," he could then be asked very specific questions about "Dr. Kim Chong-Ho." Furthermore, by having arrows already oriented with nothing on the other end, specific new questions can be formed to probe for his links in space, time, and organization.

> All leaders need some popular support for their program, particularly programs that ultimately lead to war. History shows that most leaders, even those bent on a course of aggression, rarely have made much effort to conceal their intentions, and some leaders (for example, Hitler in Mein Kampf) have provided us with virtual blueprints of what they planned to accomplish.[47]

Open-source Intelligence (OSINT) reporting is, surprisingly, the second most valuable INT in support of MDA. The interdisciplinary nature of MDA means that it requires a massive amount of context directly or indirectly linked to the target program. OSINT can provide much related background data and context when building the 6-D model.

[47] Grabo, 84.

This follows directly from the intelligence "bathtub curve" which states that the amount of available intelligence is large very early in the development of a weapon and almost as large once it is em-

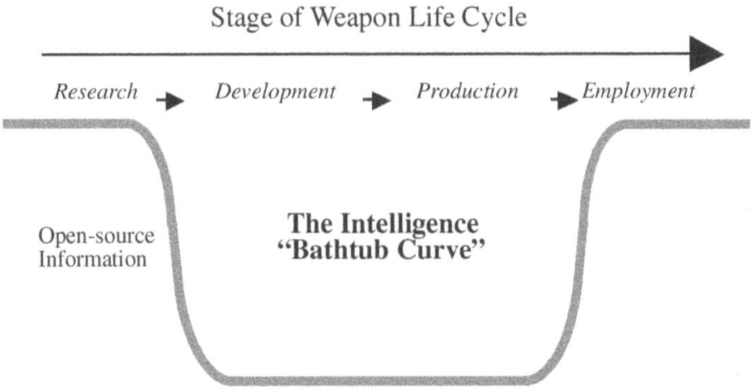

ployed, but that during the development stages done in classified programs, intelligence collection virtually dries up. For example, if an intelligence officer attended the 5th International Congress of Theoretical Physics in Washington, DC in 1938, he could have had the opportunity to interact with virtually every atomic scientist worldwide—from the U.S.'s Enrico Fermi and Albert Einstein to Germany's Werner Heisenberg—and could have asked them anything imaginable about nuclear fission. Of course, they all disappeared into classified atomic bomb programs shortly thereafter and no easy intelligence would become available until the bomb was dropped on Hiroshima.

As in this legendary case, the early stages of any WMD program are easiest to collect against and even at the "bottom of the bathtub" the key personalities have to live their lives. Thus, if an analyst can identify the key players in a WMD program, much intelligence can be gleaned by following the open-source data on the most prominent leadership likely associated with the program. During the eclipse phase, a lack of specific data—if it is taken in a proper context—can be just as valuable as positive data. Also, if a name is reported in the eclipse phase, much valuable context can be gleaned by checking the historical record. For example, a report in 1942 that Werner Heisenberg was in charge of a secret Nazi program could become much clearer by reading his presentation at the 1938 physics conference.

Building WMD requires a specific mix of personnel: strategic senior leadership to oversee the program; technical personnel to research, develop, and build the CW, BW, or nuclear payload; and technically competent logistics personnel to provide the infrastructure, order all the equipment and supplies, and pay for them.

OSINT can provide background data on the technical personnel—especially research scientists. In a small nation, there are few competent microbiologists, chemists, or nuclear physicists so that those that are available are either living dual lives; that is, working in both academic and classified programs, or by leaving a track in the open literature during their training and then subsequently disappearing from open sources. Even then, they may be absent from professional, open or "gray" literature but remain visible in their new role performing "valuable service"—of an unspecified kind—to the nation. Similarly, senior leadership is always seen in open sources, especially in Communist or totalitarian nations where the "privileged" leaders are fodder for all the propaganda journals.

> Propaganda is a very useful barometer of how concerned the country's leadership is about certain issues... Most propaganda is "true." Here we are using "truth" in a relative, not absolute sense. We mean that states cannot continually distort their objectives and policies, and particularly not to their own people. To put out totally false statements or misleading guidance is self-defeating and will not evoke the desired response.[48]

Used creatively, there are many ways that OSINT can provide meaningful context to model a WMD program using MDA.

- Coauthorship on scientific publications or presentations can be used to link scientists. Informal scientific collaborations are very important. A publication by Dr. Borisovich with a Russian coauthor or an acknowledgement in the paper for the Russian scientist sending a DNA sample is useful in defining not only who he knows but also what they both know. For tracking biologists, the Pubmed online database is very valuable because it archives titles, authors, and usually abstracts from virtually every reputable biomedical journal—including many in Russian and Chinese—from the 1960s to the present.
- Visits to meetings and conferences can be used to deduce similar information and sometimes more if a U.S. scientist has talked with the foreign scientist at the meeting.
- Visits to foreign countries often show up in the open literature of the visited nations. For example, a visit by Karjakistan's Dr. Borisovich to learn bioengineering in Italy, India, or other Western nation is likely to show up on an Italian website with meeting abstracts or an Indian website reporting research done at the Indian institute.

---

[48] Grabo, 91.

- Ceremonial occasions can be very valuable in assessing organizational relationships. For example, if the Premier of Karjakistan visited the Microbiology Institute to present Dr. Borisovich a medal for "valuable service" to the nation, one would very likely see that reported in a local journal listing all the Party dignitaries and important scientists in attendance, often with a picture of all concerned lined up in front of the building. Occasions to watch include: visits from important leaders; ground breaking or openings of new facilities; funerals; exhibitions or trade shows; and party or holiday ceremonies. Attendance by a scientist at a Party or military ceremony can be very revealing.

OSINT-directed HUMINT collection has the potential to be very valuable as the IC becomes more integrated. For example, analysis of biomedical and biotechnology open literature can:

- Identify individuals suspect in biotechnology proliferation for further HUMINT targeting.
- Identify potential HUMINT sources in the U.S. who were students or collaborators of suspect scientists who could provide important background on those scientist's expertise, travels, and other associates.
- Provide unclassified evidence of proliferation links for use in demarches. Sometimes scientific publications or news reports will indicate suspect links between nations, such as Russian scientists working in Iran, which is consistent with classified intelligence data; the unclassified source could then be used to call the attention of the foreign government to the potential proliferation issue without having to divulge classified sources.
- Provide quick screening of visa applications for suspect background in BW. "Medlining" a biologist can be done in less than a half hour in most cases. Therefore, a quick check on open-source data can rapidly indicate whether a foreign scientist is suspect and requires additional checking before granting a visa.

HUMINT- and OSINT-driven IMINT and Signals Intelligence (SIGINT) collection is likely the most valuable byproduct of the MDA approach. Much of the context required for building the multidimensional model ends up on the "cutting room floor" and never is included in finished intelligence. However, the rich context can provide very valuable clues for all the INTs. For example, IMINT is limited for WMD collection—especially BW—by the dual-use nature of WMD facilities. BW facilities are most often indistinguishable from other academic or biomedical facilities, which are in turn virtually identical to schools and warehouses. Therefore, a sketch drawn by a defector on how he walked or took the

Open-source Intelligence on Terrorist CBRNE Programs

Surprisingly OSINT can provide valuable background and context for understanding terrorist CBRNE programs. Valuable open sources on the Global War on Terrorism (GWOT) include:

News stories from reporters in-country. With the high interest level on the GWOT, many newspapers, wire services, and TV networks have sent reporters close to the action who have found unique data. Example – A Wall Street Journal reporter recovered a computer in Kabul safehouse likely used by Al Qaeda's Dr. Ayman Zawahiri which contained documents on building a chemical and biological warfare program.

Local press reports. With worldwide interest in the GWOT, press coverage in regions in which the U.S. has few collection resources can help fill in the blanks. Example – in trials in Malaysia and Indonesia, including the recent one for the suspect Bali bombers, the suspects have testified about links between Jemaah Islamiah (JI) and Al Qaeda, named the leaders involved, and identified personnel who trained in Al Qaeda camps in Afghanistan. Such news reports are posted on the Lexis/Nexis database and often can be found online on the newspapers' websites.

Official Government statements or leaked official reports. When persons are detained for questioning in the GWOT, local officials usually will release information on those detentions and sometimes other officials will talk off-the-record to local reporters. Again, these will appear in local press. Example – Pakistani government officials released statements on captured Al Qaeda members and on questioning of suspect Al Qaeda-linked nuclear scientists and physicians; Malaysian and Indonesian police released reports on suspect JI terrorists.

train from his house to visit or work at a suspect facility or a propaganda news photo of dignitaries lined up in front of a suspect facility could allow an imagery analyst to find that facility. Similarly, as mentioned above, identification that General "Joe" A heads the Missile Corps in City S and Mr. "Bob" B works for the Atomic Energy Commission in City A through HUMINT and/or OSINT could be very valuable to a SIGINT analyst who intercepts conversations between "Joe" and "Bob" about "special shipments" where the phones at each end are in the correct cities for the two offices.

Strategic Analysis of a WMD Program—How do we assemble all the data into a multi-dimensional model?

The kinds and amount of data that can potentially be used in a multidimensional analysis of a WMD program is enormous. At first glance it appears that enormous computing power plus new kinds of "data-mining" tools are necessary because of the NIMD challenge, "How do we extract Novel Intelligence from

Massive Data?" However, the Case Studies, done using only MS Word and PowerPoint as data-management tools, have indicated that MDA can surmount both NIMD challenges, massive quantities of data and too much dimensionality to the data, mainly due to the top-down approach.

The top-down modeling inherent in MDA is a way to turn perceived weaknesses of the NIMD challenge into strengths—mainly by transcending Newtonian assumptions.

WMD or CBRNE programs are strategic programs and, as described above, require the nation or terrorist organization to formulate and implement a plan that projects ahead two OODA Cycles—a Logistics Cycle to build the weapons and an Operations Cycle to field and potentially employ them. In the Logistics Cycle, the order required to build organizations to assemble WMD or CBRNE means that the plan must be implemented and remain valid for the years or decades it takes to go from conception of the plan to maturation of the infrastructure to build the WMD or CBRNE weapons, to the implementation of the plan and fielding of the weapons using that new infrastructure. Therefore, the long-range planning required in any WMD program is its greatest vulnerability to intelligence analysis. Hence the more "massive" the historical data set, the better.

BW Program Vulnerabilities to Multidimensional Analysis

- Building biological weapons requires planning that spans the entire organizational infrastructure. Leadership must coordinate people and organizations that normally do not interact.
- Key personnel include: strategic leadership, operational leadership, technical support, and logistics support.
- Materials and supplies need to be transported among facilities.
- Key persons in a BW program are professionals and usually travel.
- BW technology is virtually all dual-use.
- Research phase of weapon life cycle is open-source.

Additionally, while the problem of dual-use in all WMD programs complicates the analysis problem for WMD versus conventional programs, the dual-use nature of the programs means that considerably more data are available on those programs than might be expected. Much of a WMD program may be "hidden in plain sight" either because the dual-use really does imply two uses—that the microbiologist is making both the vaccine for legitimate health care as well as the BW agent—or is a result of denial and deception. In either case, data are available even if it is hard to interpret.

Again, more data means a better 6-D model which will be more interpretable given more data.

On the other hand, the dimensionality of the data makes its interpretation problematic. But if the methodology for building the 6-D hierarchical model is straightforward, no matter how tedious it is, it will with persistence provide better assessments.

Reconstructing a Proliferation Network

The first step in using MDA to develop a 6-D model for a WMD program is to construct a rough flow chart or timeline for the process to account for the required steps in assembling the weapon. For example, any nuclear weapons program depends on the acquisition of fissionable materials, so any flow chart for a nuclear weapons program must include either uranium enrichment or plutonium recycling from spent reactor fuel or alternative methods to buy or steal the purified elements.

Once the basic timeline is roughed out, a postulated organizational chart is constructed to account for all the technical, logistics, and operational skills required to assemble the weapon. Again, the organization may do its own research on WMD payloads or attempt to buy or steal components; the rough chart must account for all possibilities. Any intelligence that is currently available is then assessed and a very rough analysis is begun by ascribing individual "factoids" to a specific process on the timeline and/or the organization that is responsible for that process on the organization chart. The aim at this point is to be able to link key personnel or key organizations with steps on the WMD timeline. The timeline will certainly have many gaps at this point. However, if only a few key events on the timeline and the associated personnel and organizations can be identified, these few entities can be used as seeds to begin to build the 6-D model. Once a few personnel and organizations have been identified, resumes or organizational histories are constructed on them. Hopefully the timelines produced will identify a few links in the overall timeline and organizational chart. Note that maps are not very helpful at this stage because the interactions found are likely to be separated widely in both time and space.

Basic Template for Multidimensional Analysis of a BW Program

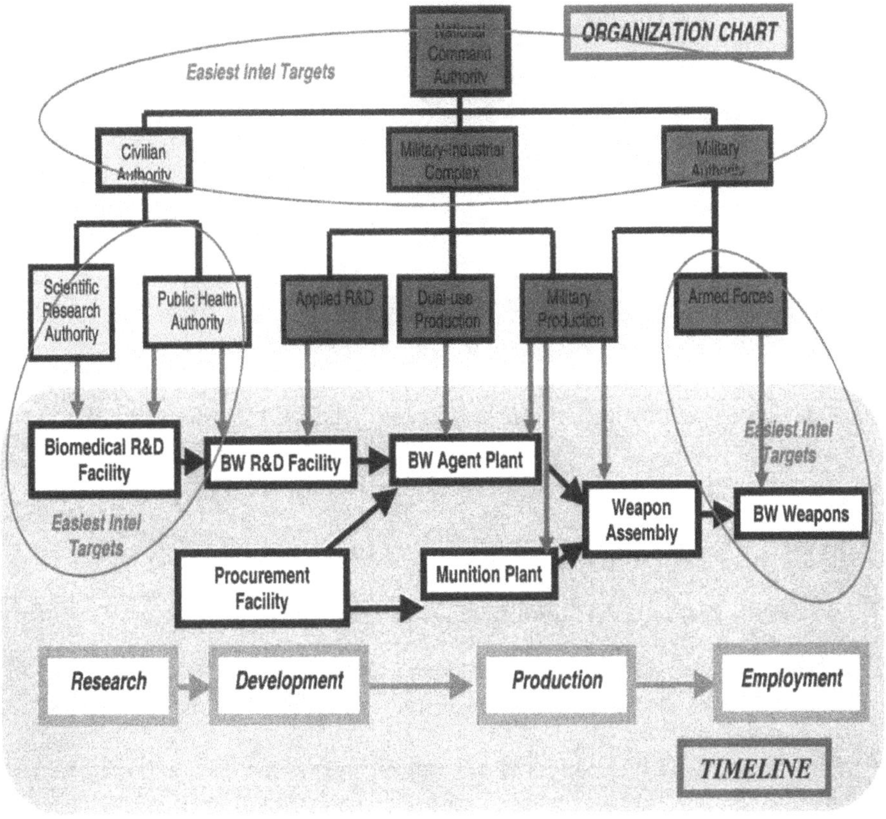

When the first pass at the known entities is complete, a systematic method to build the overall 6-D model is employed—based on the intelligence "bathtub" curve. Since it is very likely that most data can be obtained about the first and last steps in the overall process and about the most visible leadership, those entities are targeted and the organizational infrastructure is investigated in detail—without much regard to whether the data are directly linked to WMD. For example:

- If it was determined that the Babool Microbiology Institute was potentially involved in BW, its history would be built to include as many personnel and projects as could be determined from all sources.
- If it was learned that the Institute was subordinate to the Karjakistan Ministry of Health, a history would be built on the Ministry, to include its subordination, leadership, and its subordinate organizations.

- If it was learned that the Karjakistani Army employs SCUD missiles (which have been reported to be CW- or BW-capable in other nations, a rough history of the Karjakistani SCUD program would be built to determine when the program started, if the missiles are home-built or bought, and any indications of which military units employ them.

The aim of the MDA at this point is to begin to fill in the overall diagram to provide context for the national organization. One begins by studying entities top-down by looking for the processes they are involved in, such as dual-use research or procurement of missile systems. As reports are found and a resume or entity history is built, one can begin bottom-up modeling to assemble the subordinate entities into a unit, where the focus is on scientists, equipment, materials, and processes occurring inside a particular facility. Every time any entity is characterized, its 6-D model will provide clues on where to look next since one can either drill down to its subordinate entities and processes or build up the more general process and organization of which it is a part.

Multidimensional Analysis of WMD Programs – Lessons Learned

- **FOLLOW THE PEOPLE**... They will lead you to the projects.
- Resumes of key people are critical.
- **HISTORY IS IMPORTANT**... You cannot know where they're going until you know where they've been.
- Relationship of organizational chart to timeline is critical.
- Facilities are processes on a timeline as well as boxes that enclose organizations.

The major lesson learned from using MDA on several BW and CBRNE programs is that Multidimensional Analysis techniques are not difficult and they do not require extensive computing power. BUT they are tedious because one needs to build an entire overview of the target nation's infrastructure and leadership to pick out the parts that are involved in WMD or CBRNE. AND they take an enormous amount of time and reading. For example, the MDA project on North Korean BW has been in place for almost three years and a first pass at all the pertinent reporting has not yet been completed. However, the benefits are already great. From the detailed 6-D model the warning analyst using MDA can do several things that conventional methodologies have difficulty doing.

Multidimensional Analysis for Strategic Warning in a World of WMD and Terrorism

MDA can provide strategic warning in a world of WMD and terrorism. Since a timeline is the core plot of MDA, by building knowledge of where the WMD program came from and when key events happened in the past, the warning analyst can provide critical assessments of where it might go in the future. Most importantly, MDA can provide warning on a WMD program *before* the weapons are actually built; that is, it can provide intelligence on what the adversary's new strategic infrastructure will look like before it is built. In short, using MDA, a warning analyst can give strategic warning—even in a world of WMD and terrorism.

MDA can provide very specific information for targeting collection. As described above, feedback to collectors is critical for building a complete 6-D model, and the detailed model of every entity in the model provides context for new collection.

MDA can provide specific assessments on intelligence gaps. In MDA, intelligence gaps become very clear. Entities that are virtually unfilled—large holes—on the 6-D models are cause for concern. However, as the model fills up around them, the analyst can construct a rather detailed model of what needs to be collected. For example, if the Babool Microbiology Institute was built in 1984 and research began there on anthrax in collaboration with Dr. Borisovich the next year, one can project that somewhere in the late 1980s one can look for efforts to build production fermenters—either by the military or for biopesticides or for vaccines. Projecting forward or back in time—either for projects along the timeline or for key personnel up or down the organizational ladder—can be very useful in determining where to look next to fill the gaps.

> ... it is usually more important to understand the strategic importance of the particular issue to the nation than it is to place undue weight on traditional behavior and priorities.[49]

MDA can also provide a mechanism to help screen out mirror-imaging in assessments or relying on remembered thoughts on a nation's priorities, and by doing so, it gives some indication of whether gaps are really gaps or something else. For example, we might assess that a nation would be stupid to use manned aircraft to deliver BW agents over a battlefield and that covert employment by Special Forces might be a better way to attack U.S. troops in the field. If there is

---

[49]Grabo, 86.

reporting to fill in the "aircraft delivery" process on the timeline but none on the Special Forces delivery process, it could be assessed as (1) a gap in intelligence, (2) excellent denial and deception by the adversary, or (3) a true lack of Special Forces delivery. In MDA the analyst can begin to assess which is true by related organizational or personal data such as aircraft unit training in suicide operations, vaccinations for some units but not others, visits by biologists to certain units, or subordination of either unit to strategic commands rather than the normal tactical channels. Given the multiple linkages in time and organization of any part of a WMD program to another, some kind of linkage should become available even given denial and deception.

> Power talks. Realistic descriptions of the buildup of military power often convey a better sense of the likelihood of action than will a series of estimative judgments which fail to include the military details or reasons on which the assessment is based. To understand the capability, and to be able to view it objectively, is a prerequisite to the understanding of intent.[50]

MDA can help assess "Why?" "Who?" "What?" "When?" "Where?" "Why?" and "How?" Conventional methods of intelligence analysis that concentrate on weaponry and facilities can address "What" and "Where," but have difficulty in assessing the rest. We have shown MDA can directly address all the remaining questions required to write a good story except "Why?"

Assessing "Why" is clearly the most difficult question for any warning analyst because it requires "getting inside the adversary's head" to deduce his or her intentions. The major difficulty lies in that currently any assessment of intent must be built totally on others' assessments of intent. Usually assessments of intent come from a source stating that he heard the target leader say something. Even if the statement was, "I plan to build a BW program," the statement may not provide a true assessment: the source may have heard a statement that was different and interpreted to be the one given; or the leader could have uttered the statement but not meant what he said; or the leader could have meant what he said but may not have been able to make good on the plan for many reasons.

While MDA does account for such statements in building assessments, it also can provide independent assessment of the intent. If the leader really was going to build a BW program, those words would produce many more words in many different venues involving planning conferences followed by organizational meetings...straight through all the steps in the timeline. Was the statement made

---

[50]Grabo, 24.

at an appropriate place in the timeline? Were those present the appropriate leaders in the organization which would carry out the order? Most important, does the infrastructure provide the capability assessed and is that capability consistent with a plan and the historical record of how the program was built?

MDA can assess intent by actions rather than words. By building a timeline for a potential WMD program one can project dual-use agent or payload programs with parallel munitions programs and later compare production and employment reporting with previous knowledge on how the project did the R&D for the assessed weapons and with present knowledge of how the project is doing the R&D for the next generation of weapons.

All those processes require planning. Planning shows intent. Assessing intent—"why" someone is doing something—is crucial to strategic warning.

Chapter 10

MODELING HOW WE MODEL

How can we provide strategic analysis to build our own strategic plan? Step 2 in building Warning Analysis for the Information Age is to model how we think —build and test hypotheses—to provide strategic warning so that we can then develop tools to help automate the process.

From Responding Faster to Thinking Smarter—Strategic Analysis for the Information Age

> Our U.S. defense strategy seeks new levels of effectiveness by harnessing the power of advanced technologies. A central premise to future military strategy is the formation of a system of systems (SOS) to attain dominant battlespace knowledge. By coalescing data from collection and processing systems, the resulting information can be integrated with systems of weaponry and warriors for a seamless sensor-to-shooter flow. Linking these with the capabilities of maneuver, strike, logistics, and protection will allow decisionmakers at every level to respond significantly faster than any adversary and in any operational situation.[51]

Virtually every discussion of "harnessing the power of advanced technologies" ultimately comes down to defining the most critical thing that new technologies will ultimately allow us to do. And the answer is invariably that we will be able to "respond faster." That answer is certainly correct, but it can be very misleading if we are still thinking tactically in the Newtonian, Industrial-Age paradigm.

//

- Idea of fast transients suggests that, in order to win, we should operate at a *faster tempo or rhythm* than our adversaries—or, better yet, get inside the adversary's *Observation-Orientation-Decision-Action time cycle or loop.*
- Why? Such activity will make us appear ambiguous (unpredictable) thereby generate *confusion* and *disorder* among our adversaries—since our adversaries will be *unable* to generate mental images or pictures that agree with the *menacing* as well as *faster* transient rhythm or patterns they are competing against.[52]

//

---

[51] Annette J. Krygiel, *Behind the Wizard's Curtain: An Integration Environment for a System of Systems* (Washington D.C., National Defense University, 1999), 1.

[52] Col Boyd.

When Col Boyd formulated the Decision Cycle concept for military operational planning, he was defining how to integrate thinking and acting for optimal unit performance. One of the major implications of his model is the notion of thinking "inside the adversary's Decision Cycle," that is, if you can complete your Decision Cycle faster than your opponent can complete his, you will have the advantage.

Inherent in this concept are two points: (1) the better one can observe, orient, and make a plan, the more effective his cycle will become, and (2) the faster one can execute that plan, the more efficient his cycle will become. However, as indicated before, the most effective organization for intelligence (observing and orienting) is a network that provides informed inaction whereas the most efficient organization for operations (deciding and acting) is a hierarchy that provides uninformed action.

Therefore, every organization has to negotiate a tradeoff. Do I want to be very smart and very slow or do I want to be very powerful, very fast, and very stupid? If I take the time to understand all the intelligence and come up with the best possible plan I will never accomplish anything, but if I build only a single plan that I can execute seamlessly and rapidly I may accomplish the wrong thing.

The Cold War could be approximated by a two-player-zero-sum game where linear Newtonian, Industrial-Age thinking would suffice. As we have seen, the result was a single integrated "strategic" plan that could be instantly put into motion...and organizational thinking channeled to the "very powerful and very fast" option.

But in a Post-Cold War multi-player non-zero-sum-game, Newtonian thinking is obsolete. "Very powerful and very fast" also is likely to be very stupid. In the Information Age, one wins principally by being smarter than the adversary. BUT how can one be smart and still be fast? After all, the object is still to be able to "think inside" the adversary's Decision Cycle.

Fast is a relative thing. If one is thinking tactically, fast is a matter of sensing the coming attack and responding faster than the adversary. If one is thinking strategically, fast is a matter of sensing the world, the adversary, and oneself and coming up with a new plan for a new infrastructure that is more effective than the opponent's, then building and employing that new infrastructure faster than the adversary can counter.

Strategic thinking and strategic planning go out to the *next* Decision Cycle. The most effective organization is one that can execute the current plan as rapidly and efficiently as possible ***while simultaneously rebuilding itself for a new plan.***

Building any new infrastructure is by nature very slow. For example, building any WMD from scratch takes years. On a strategic time scale, "fast" is like watching a glacier move. Therefore, a strategic plan must be "smart." If our *next generation* organization and tools are smarter and more effective than the adversary's, they will prevail.

> In tactical thinking, faster is better. In strategic thinking, smarter is better.

Therefore, to provide strategic warning for strategic thinking we need to rebuild ourselves for a strategic war on terrorism and WMD proliferation—even as we fight a tactical war against terrorist acts and WMD proliferation. To do this we must both build new tools to be able to think more effectively and reorient our organizational thinking to provide for strategic warning and planning.

Hypothesis Testing as an OODA Cycle—Thinking about How We Think

> It is readily apparent that a determination of the order-of-battle (OB) of foreign forces is of decisive importance for warning intelligence. Indeed, insofar as warning rests on a determination of the facts—as opposed to the more complex problem of determining what the facts mean and issuing some interpretive judgment—the order-of-battle facts will often be the single most important element in warning.[53]

Determining the order-of-battle of foreign forces is a part of thinking strategically. By determining what forces an adversary is building, one can project what kind of force structure he is planning. Plans define logistics, but logistics also reflect the plans. Multidimensional Analysis (MDA) provides a systematic way to define an adversary's WMD order-of-battle. What WMD does he have? What WMD is he trying to build? From that knowledge one can project what WMD he is planning to build. The major difference from a standard OB is that a WMD OB includes dual-use industries, organizations, leaders, scientists, and engineers.

> The best judgments do not necessarily result from bringing more people into the assessment process, and particularly those who are familiar with all the available infotmation. The most accurate warning judgments often are made by a minority of individuals. The coming of most conflicts is much longer term than most people believe, and the first indications of the approaching crisis are often received (if not discerned) months before the conflict erupts. As a research

[53] Grabo, 55.

> problem, warning involves an in-depth, cumulative compiling and analysis of these trends and developments rather than an excessive concentration on the latest or most current information, which can be highly misleading.[54]

MDA follows directly from Cynthia Grabo's assessment on warning intelligence. History matters. Knowing the history of what weapons of mass destruction are being researched, developed, and built provides the baseline for strategic analysis and is the basis for strategic warning. But unless we can model our own thought processes in building Multidimensional Analysis (MDA) or strategic warning, we cannot hope to write a computer algorithm to automate the process. How do we do that? Again, Grabo provides the critical clue.

> As a *research problem*, warning involves an in-depth, cumulative compiling and analysis of these trends and developments...[55]

MDA or strategic warning is a research problem. First and foremost, every intelligence analyst is a researcher.

As indicated before, the problem of Iraq's WMD is not different from my eighth-grade daughter's inventions project, or any research for that matter. And the core of all critical research is hypothesis testing. Of course, hypothesis testing is done in response to asking a question. Who? What? When? Where? Why? How? Subsequently, research is built on its own Decision Cycle:

- ***Hypothesis*** — Build a possible mechanism for how the world works and define an experiment to test the hypothesis.
- ***Experiment*** — Perform a series of interactions with the world and collect data.
- ***Observation*** — Observe the data.
- ***Hypothesis*** — Correlate the data with that predicted by the hypothesis; keep hypotheses that are supported by the data, and discard hypotheses that are inconsistent with the data.
- *Repeat above.*
- ***Theory*** — After enough experiments are performed to give a high degree of credence to a given hypothesis, it moves up to being a "theory."

---

[54] Grabo, 162.
[55] Grabo, 162.

The only difference between the scientific method, the researcher's Decision Cycle, and the OODA Cycle is the ordering of events.

Research

[Hypothesis	Define Experiment	Experiment	Observation	Hypothesis] or Theory

Military

[Orientation	Decision	Action]	[Observation	Orientation]

For the military officer, the most important step is the action taken against the adversary and, therefore, the OODA cycle culminates in that action. For the researcher, the most important step is the Theory, and, therefore, the Hypothesis Testing cycle culminates with a better hypothesis and ultimately a theory.

For the military officer, taking the action is paramount. For the researcher, building a plan for future action is paramount.

For the military officer, actions are collection-driven. For the researcher, actions are hypothesis-driven.

The crucial step in answering the original question is the orientation step where the hypothesis is compared against observed data. The researcher's major task is to build a hypothesis that answers the question in a way that is consistent with all the data. For the military officer, this is not an issue because the decision-maker has already determined which hypothesis answers the question and which plan can implement that hypothesis; current intelligence is comparing new data with the plan to ensure that it is still on course and/or any contingencies in the plan are addressed.

The current intelligence analyst's Decision Cycle is a classical OODA cycle because actionable assessments for implementing current plan are the goal. Therefore, current intelligence is collection-driven.

- ***Observe*** the incoming reporting.
- ***Orient*** the reporting to the current plan and assess its implications for action according to that plan.
- ***Decide*** what is most important to report for current action.
- ***Act*** by reporting an assessment to the decisionmaker.

However, the warning analyst's Decision Cycle must be more like the researcher's because the goal of the warning analyst is to providing actionable assessments for building a new plan. Therefore, warning analysis is hypothesis-driven.

- ***Orient*** (Hypothesize) using all the current data built into a 6-D multi-layer model of the adversary.
- ***Decide*** (Build an experiment) on what needs to be collected to test the hypothesis.
- ***Act*** (Experiment) by retrieving reporting from available databases and libraries or, if necessary, directing new collection.
- ***Observe*** the collected data.
- ***Orient*** (Assess) the newly examined data against the hypothesis.
- ***Orient*** (Assess) whether the hypothesis is a theory.
  If not Repeat above.
  If so,
- ***Act*** by reporting the assessment and potential new plan to the policymaker.

Strategic analysis and warning is hypothesis-driven. MDA is hypothesis-driven. Therefore, to model how the strategic analyst should model the world—and therefore to decide what kinds of tools he or she might need—we need to investigate the steps in hypothesis testing.

Good strategic analysis ultimately addresses the fundamental questions that began the research. Who is building a WMD program? What weapons is he building? Where is he building them? When and where does he plan to use them? How will they be employed? Why has he taken this particular strategy? As indicated before, by linking entities in space, time, and organization, MDA builds charts that show the history of the WMD program in such terms. To provide strategic warning, the MDA analyst needs to chart the WMD program in 6-D, then interpret the results to address the customers' questions.

What is fascinating in this respect is that the questions and their answers are virtually always linear and the customers want to hear the linear answer in the form of a story. The warning analyst then needs to become a storyteller, picking out a particular thread from the 6-D map to communicate to the customer. This is very similar to the role of the navigator on board ship. The navigator plots the ship on a map versus all the rocks and shoals and picks out the best course toward the goal. This is because the customer, like the ship's Captain, needs to answer the same set of questions about his own ship. Who am I going to meet? What is my mission? When do I start? Where to I plot my course? How do I implement the plan? Why is that important?

Whether taking observations and comparing them with the current hypothesis or map or taking the hypothesis or map and deciding the plan, the orientation process is not complete until the 6-D analysis becomes a linear story that plots a best guess trajectory or vector for both ourselves and our adversaries in that 6-D hypothesis or worldview.

From Hypothesis to Theory—
Building a Theory on Building a Theory

There are several steps a researcher performs in going from observations of the world or from collected data to knowledge of the world and the ability to transmit that knowledge to build an actionable plan.

The core of scientific research has always been hypothesis testing. This continues to be true in the Information Age, but the way scientists build and test hypotheses is changing markedly with our ability to generate, store, and recall massive quantities of data.

From Paper-World Research to Cyber-World Research

The scientist builds a hypothesis and tests that hypothesis by analyzing current data and coming up with a theory of how the world works that is supported by that data. He or she formulates experiments to test that hypothesis, performs those experiments, and then compares the results of the experiments with those expected according to the hypothesis. If the experimental results are consistent with the hypothesis, the hypothesis can then be refined and tested further with new and different experiments. This series of hypothesis testing steps continues to refine the hypothesis, and when enough experimental tests have been performed, and the data support the hypothesis sufficiently well, the scientist can consider the hypothesis to be a theory.

In the past—through the Industrial Age—these steps were invariably done sequentially:

Hypothesis

Formulate Experiment

Perform Experiment

Compare Experiment and Hypothesis

Refine Hypothesis

In the Information Age, the scientific method remains the same with a single modification—the timing of the cycle. The enormous rate at which data are being collected and archived in databases means that hypothesis testing can be done uncoupled from laboratory experimentation or intelligence collection. Additionally, previously collected scientific and intelligence data are also archived in a format in which it can now easily be accessed and recalled. Therefore, bioinformatics is based on a new twist on the scientific method. A scientist can now formulate a hypothesis, formulate an experiment to test that hypothesis, but before going into the lab ask, "Has anyone already done that experiment?" He or she can then check all available databases and, if the experiment has already been done, use those experimental results to test the hypothesis. An intelligence analyst should be able to do the same; using MDA to understand intelligence reports parallels the use of bioinformatics to understand biological data.

Information-Age biology has changed the scientific method slightly by decoupling hypothesis testing and experimentation. A biologist can now do hypothesis testing based on data archived in the many available databases. Therefore, in the Information Age, the experimental and hypothesis-testing components of the scientific method can be separate:

Experimental Cycle

Formulate Experimental Protocol

Perform Experiment on one genome/ organism

Archive data in database

Check database for completeness

Move to new genome/organism

Information Cycle

Hypothesis

Formulate Experiment

Recall Experimental Results from Database

Compare Experiment and Hypothesis

Refine Hypothesis

Similarly, an intelligence analyst can now do hypothesis testing based on data archived in the many available databases. In the Information Age the collection and hypothesis-testing components of the analytical method can be separate:

Collection Cycle

Formulate Collection Requirements Protocol
 Collect intelligence on a given target
  Archive data in database
   Check database for completeness
    Move to new target

Information Cycle

Hypothesis
 Formulate Evidence Needed to Test Hypothesis
  Recall Reports from Database
   Compare Reports and Hypothesis
    Refine Hypothesis

It is only when there is no experimental result or intelligence report available in any database that the Information-age biologist or analyst needs to actually go into the lab to perform an experiment or go into the field to collect new intelligence.

Bioinformatics, Multidimensional Analysis and Hypothesis Testing for the Information Age

In any kind of research project there is a series of steps the researcher takes from the formulation of a research problem to the publication of a theory with supporting experimental results. An intelligence analyst performs the identical series of steps from the identification of an intelligence question to the publication of an assessment with supporting intelligence reports. And both the biologists and analysts are splitting their hypothesis testing the way historians have done for decades.

Historians perform two kinds of research: (1) collection and documentation of historical artifacts and records, and (2) analysis based on the collected documentation. For example, a historian studying the American Civil War could choose to go to a historic battlefield site and dig for new artifacts or search for new evidence in the personal effects saved by descendants of historical figures. Sometimes, if the era being investigated is recent such as World War II, the historian could interview participants themselves. This type of historical research is

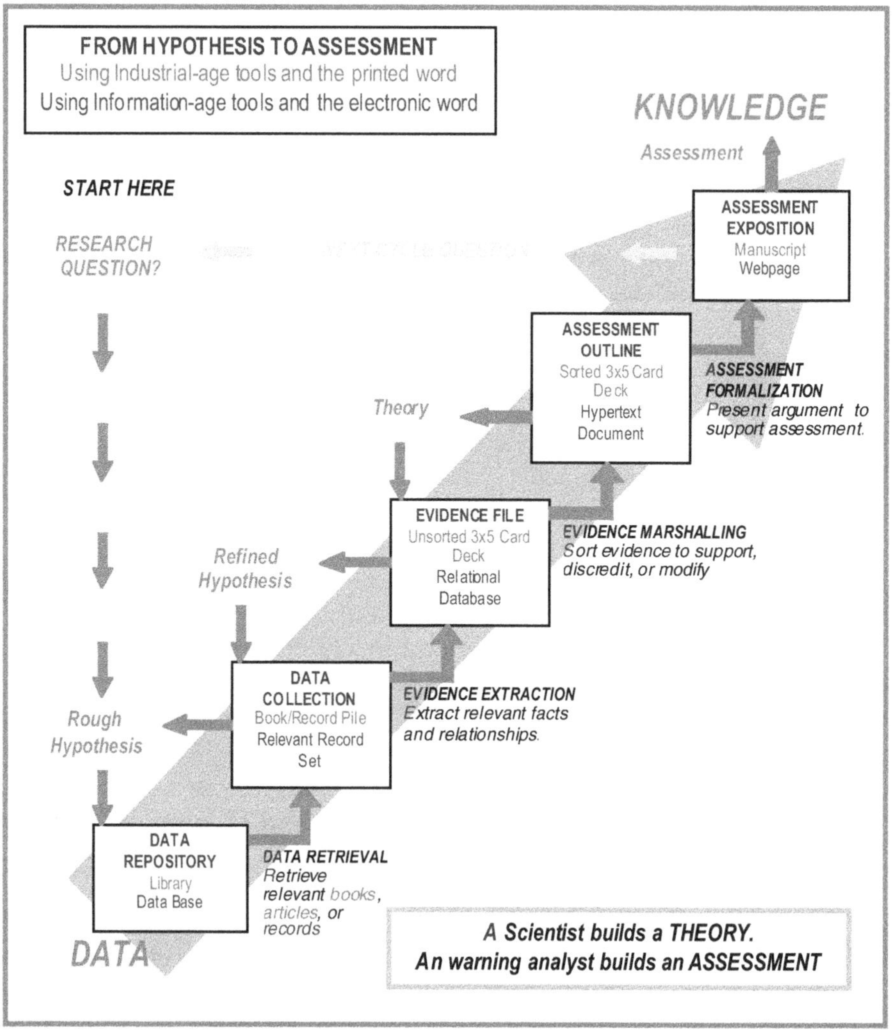

in many ways similar to the biologists' experimental method of hypothesis testing or to the classical intelligence collection cycle. However, some historians never collect artifacts themselves but rather use libraries to dig through documentation and records to develop new insights into historical events. Sometimes the records are primary evidence, such as court records or archives of government agencies, but often the records are books published by other authors.

With the advent of automated data collection, biological researchers and the Intelligence Community are both amassing archives in databases similar to historical archives stored in libraries. Therefore, the methodologies of bioinformatics and intelligence analysis will ultimately have more in common with a historian's library research than the traditional experimental or collection approach.

At some time in school, we learned to do historical library research. The methodology used in that kind of research can serve as a model for the kind of thinking and methods that can prove fruitful in both bioinformatics and intelligence analysis. We only need to update the approach from using libraries, printed documents, and 3"x5" index cards to using databases, electronic records, and data manipulation tools. The strategies and hypothesis testing methods we learned in library research are very applicable to bioinformatics and Information-Age intelligence.

> ***hypothesis. n. ... 2.*** *A proposition or principle put forth or stated (without any reference to its correspondence with fact) merely as a basis for reasoning or argument, or as a premise from which to draw a conclusion; a supposition.*
>
> The Oxford English Dictionary

Data Retrieval. When a research question is asked or a research problem is addressed, the first step is to form a preliminary hypothesis that can provide an answer to that question. Then, using that preliminary hypothesis, the researcher goes to the data repository to retrieve records relevant to the question at hand to build a data collection.

The purpose of this step is to collect records relevant to the hypothesis or problem. The researcher now has a data collection—or "shoebox"—that contains records for further evaluation, some directly and some which may not be looked at until this step is repeated for a new or modified hypothesis after testing the original one.

- *Industrial-Age Methodology.* The researcher went to the library and, by using catalogs and indices, retrieved books and documents relevant to the problem. These were taken home or set aside for future use.
- *Information-Age Methodology.* The researcher logs onto the Internet, online library, or database and using Boolean search tools identifies and retrieves records relevant to the problem. These are then downloaded and set aside for future use.

The value-added in building the data collection is that the researcher has a local dataset that contains records relevant to the question or problem. As he or she extracts evidence and builds cases for various hypotheses, this dataset—a "shoebox" full of valuable "stuff"—is a very important resource to use to find new evidence as hypotheses are discarded, modified, or built.

evidence. n. ... 5. Grounds for belief; testimony or facts tending to prove or disprove any conclusion.

The Oxford English Dictionary

Evidence Extraction. When a sufficient data collection is amassed, the researcher reads the relevant records and extracts bits of evidence[56] pertinent to the problem at hand. At this point, if it becomes clear that the first pass on data retrieval did not collect all the necessary relevant records, the researcher can use new keywords obtained to do another round of data retrieval. The extracted evidence then is stored in an evidence file.

The purpose of this step is to find all the bits of data—often called "factoids" or "nuggets"—that can serve as evidence to test, support, discredit, or modify the hypothesis at hand. The hypotheses can be very general, "All North Korean microbiologists are potentially involved in a BW program," or very specific, "Dr. Kim Chong-Ho is producing anthrax starter cultures for weaponization." It is important to remember that evidence is a collection of "testimony or facts" that support or discredit a hypothesis. Therefore, evidence extraction is highly dependent on the hypothesis at hand and will produce a differing result when done with respect to a new or modified hypothesis.

- *Industrial-Age Methodology.* The researcher read the relevant books and documents in the "shoebox" and looked for individual facts and ideas that could be used as evidence to support, reject, or modify the hypothesis. These were copied on 3x5 cards—one to a card along with referencing information. The cards were then set aside for future analysis.
- *Information-Age Methodology.* The researcher reads the relevant records in the electronic "shoebox" and does a "cut and paste" of individual facts and data that can be tied to the hypothesis. If the final dataset is expected to be small, these evidence "nuggets" can be copied into a word-processing file—along with referencing information.

[56]As indicated here, I define "evidence" as data that is pertinent to the problem at hand. As such, "evidence" is always linked with a hypothesis. For example, for GEN Eisenhower on 5 June 1944, the barometric pressure in England or California was just data, but the barometric pressure in Iceland was evidence to be weighed in support of the hypothesis that a low barometric reading in Iceland on 5 June argues bad weather in the English Channel on 6 June. And of course, the barometric pressure/bad weather hypothesis was only valid for GEN Eisenhower in addressing the question, "Do I invade tomorrow or not?" The implication here is that not all data in a data repository is "evidence." It only becomes "evidence" after it is collected and judged relevant then sorted and judged pertinent to the hypothesis at hand.

If the final dataset is expected to be large, the researcher will set up a relational database and store the evidence "nuggets" as individual entries in the relational database.

The value-added in building the evidence file or unsorted 3x5 card deck is that evidence "nuggets" relevant to the hypotheses at hand are available to evaluate those hypotheses directly and also any future modified or new hypotheses. For example, a report that "Dr. Kim Chong-Ho is an expert on botulinum toxin" may be used to discredit the hypothesis that he is producing anthrax cultures, to support the hypothesis that he is overseeing a botulinum toxin BW program, or merely to back up a hypothesis that he is a well-versed microbiologist. However, keeping this "nugget" in the evidence file allows the researcher to go back to test these or new hypotheses without having to start from the data collection step every time. In MDA, evidence can link entities in 6-D and at multiple hierarchical levels; evidence that may lead to a dead end for one hypothesis may be very useful to test another.

> ***theory. n. ... 4.a.*** *A scheme or system of ideas or statements held as an explanation or account of a group of facts or phenomena; a hypothesis that has been confirmed or established by observation or experiment, and is propounded or accepted accounting for the known facts; a statement of what are held to be general laws, principles, or causes of something known or observed.*
>
> The Oxford English Dictionary

Evidence Marshalling. When enough evidence has been extracted and stored in an evidence file, the researcher builds a case to argue for a hypothesis using the individual pieces of evidence in the file.

If not enough evidence is in the file on a particular topic, the researcher can use new keywords or Boolean combinations of keywords to perform another round of data retrieval and evidence extraction to build the evidence file. An important point to remember here is that the evidence file is unsorted data while the evidence marshalling procedure sorts and re-orders that evidence to build a coherent logical story in support of a hypothesis. At this point the theory or assessment exposition will have ideas, facts, experimental data, or intelligence reports to support it.

Further, for the sake of expediency and based on academic principle, the preferred method of performing analysis is grounded in the principles espoused by the curriculum of the Joint Military Intellligence College and encompassing the suggested guidance and models of MacEachin, Heuer, Toulmin, Schum, and Hughes.[57]

> These models of critical thinking move beyond the simplistic and intuitive, representing higher-order cognitive function and the ability to replicate and illustrate the analytical process. They include Analysis of Competing Hypotheses (ACH) methods, the use of evidence and inference, argumentation, and other techniques employing "imaginative and critical reasoning."[58]

> The second O, orientation—as the repository of our genetic heritage, cultural tradition, and previous experiences—is the most important part of the O-O-D-A loop since it shapes the way we observe, the way, we decide, the way we act.[59]
>
> Col Boyd

Orientation is built on hypothesis testing. How we can integrate our "genetic heritage, cultural tradition, and previous experience" into models that systematize that worldview for Decisionmaking is the key challenge for the IC of the 21st Century. Therefore, research into analyzing how we analyze is critical for computer-assisted implementation of strategic analysis. We cannot program a computer to help us think until we know how we think—in detail. The first step toward that goal is the understanding that analysis is research, that hypothesis testing is the OODA Cycle, and that going into the Information Age, it is the Orientation step of the national OODA Cycle that is broken.

Theory Formulation. When the hypothesis has been examined and evidence marshaled to test the hypothesis, the researcher can now propose a new theory—based on facts and experimental evidence or intelligence reporting.

The purpose of this step is to provide a "published" version of the theory as a story that presents a hypothesis and the evidence that supports (or questions) it. At this point, dependent on the completeness of the evidence supporting the the-

---

[57] These refer to proponents of new methodologies analytical reasoning through study of the analytical process: Douglas J. MacEachin, Richards J. Heuer, Stephen E. Toulmin, Dr. David A. Schum, and Francis J. Hughes. I should note that the concept of Bottom-Up data-driven modeling versus Top-Down hypothesis-driven modeling is virtually identical to Heuer's distinction between data-driven analysis and concept-driven analysis. A reading list of their works can be found in Rue (ref below).

[58] GYSGT Steven S. Rue, USMC, *The Breakdown of the PC Paradigm: Information Display Technology As as Analysis Inhibitor*, MSSI Thesis (Washington, D.C: Joint Military Intelligence College, August 2003), 12.

[59] Col Boyd.

ory, the researcher could dip back into the evidence file or go all the way back to the data repository for additional evidence to build the case. If the evidence was incomplete at that point, the researcher would be required to propose and perform new experiments or collect additional intelligence for further test of the theory. If a new evidence "nugget" is found that apparently discredits the current hypothesis or theory, the scientist or analyst can return to the evidence file with a modified or totally new hypothesis which can then be rapidly tested against the evidence already available, albeit in an unsorted fashion with respect to the new hypothesis. The ability of being able to re-sort evidence file or "3x5 cards" to test or re-test a hypothesis more than overweighs the time and energy expended in building and maintaining the evidence file.[60]

The value-added in theory formulation is that the researcher has taken a systematic methodology to collect data and extract evidence that directly supports or discredits hypotheses. A scientist will usually wait until enough iterations of the Hypothesis Testing Cycle have been completed to support the theory at hand unequivocally before publishing. An intelligence analyst often will not have that luxury, but a systematic hypothesis testing approach, especially when multiple competing hypotheses are tested simultaneously with the same evidence file, can provide the analyst the ability to publish his or her assessment at almost any time, either as a brief or paper. However, with fewer iterations of the cycle, the assessment may need to provide more than one hypothesis with both supporting and discrediting evidence for each.

I suggest that the basic methodology of data retrieval and evidence marshalling in support of hypothesis testing has not changed and will not change as the biological and intelligence communities go from the Industrial Age with the printed word and library to the Information Age with the electronic word and database—only that the methodology will get much more powerful as more data become available along with tools to identify, retrieve, and order evidence.

---

[60] The concept of the "evidence file" or "electronic 3x5 card deck" can be directly linked to analytical methodologies such as Analysis of Competing Hypotheses (ACH) or other methods of using evidence and inference. The "evidence file" is the analyst's unsorted "3x5 card deck" of data that he or she has collected because it appears to be pertinent to the question at hand. Accordingly, if using ACH as an analytical tool, the analyst can sort the "3x5 cards" once for each of the competing hypotheses to support, discredit, or modify each in turn for further comparison. The power in MDA in this process is that a massive amount of evidence is compiled on the basis of very generic models such as the basic WMD timeline and organization chart which then can be used directly as an evidence file for systematic hypothesis testing tools such as ACH.

Using Homology Searching in Intelligence Analysis

In the biological sciences another kind of powerful tool for evidence evaluation is called homology comparison or homology searching. It has the potential for use in Information-Age strategic analysis. Homology searching is based on the theory that organisms grow and develop through gene networks that program all the biochemical steps in that process and that the genes in the program are inherited directly or with slight changes (or mutations) from their ancestors and parents. MDA of several WMD programs suggests that WMD programs grow and develop on the basis of organizational networks that define all the scientific, technical, and leadership steps in that process and that the people in the program acquire the knowledge and skills directly from their scientific or leadership mentors.

Gene networks program development of biological organisms. People networks develop WMD programs.

Gene traits are inherited from ancestors and parents. Scientific, technical, and leadership traits are learned from mentors.

Once again, history matters.

Following gene pedigrees can help geneticists and molecular biologists to understand organismal development and disease. Following mentorship pedigrees can help warning analysts to understand organizational development and WMD programs.

MDA builds a top-down graphical hypothesis of the steps and organizations required for a WMD program. When MDA has been done on several WMD programs, comparison among the related WMD models can provide important clues for further analysis and collection in the same way that homology searching in genetics and molecular biology is becoming a very powerful bioinformatics tool in the study of organismal development and disease. Biologists use "model" organisms, such as yeast, fruit flies, mice, and worms, to study human development and disease because the gene networks in all those organisms are related not only in function but also in pedigree—common genes from common ancestors. Such a methodology can also be very powerful in studying WMD development because the people networks in WMD programs worldwide are related not only in function but often in pedigree—common technologies from common proliferators and mentors.

Identification of homology between genes can be used as evidence or as a guide for further experimentation. The search for homology between WMD personnel can also be fruitful when several programs can be compared using MDA. This is done in four major ways.

- *Comparison of disease genes with normal genes in the same organism.* By comparing the gene sequences and structures of a mutated gene in a disease patient and the same gene in a normal person, molecular biologists can deduce the molecular differences in the DNA and proteins that cause the malfunction in the disease. Example: sickle cell human beta-hemoglobin vs. normal human beta-hemoglobin. Similarly, by comparing the resumes of WMD-associated leaders, scientists, and engineers with those of "normal" personnel working in legitimate dual-use programs in the same country, warning analysts can begin to build profiles and indicators for the differences expected in going from legitimate dual-use programs to WMD programs.
- *Comparison of related genes in the same organism.* Often there are gene families in an organism that encode homologous but not identical protein sequences. Example: human alpha-hemoglobin and beta-hemoglobin expressed in adults vs. delta-hemoglobin and epsilon-hemoglobin expressed in infants and fetuses. The homology is evidence that those proteins have similar functions, but biologists can then deduce fine differences in the differing genes that function in different places in the body or at different times in development. Potentially, comparison of WMD personnel resumes and organizational histories with resumes and histories in legitimate dual-use programs can point to places or times where the two diverge.
- *Comparison of the same gene in related organisms.* Highly homologous proteins in different organisms often have the same function. Example: human beta-globin vs. mouse beta-globin. Comparison of WMD personnel resumes and organizational histories in one state with those in other WMD-developing countries to indicate emergent WMD programs. This can be even more powerful in cases where the personnel of one nation have been actively proliferating WMD to the second nation, because knowledge of the first nation's WMD program will provide very specific I&W on the second nation's WMD program.
- *Comparison of related genes in related organisms.* Homologous proteins in different organisms often have similar functions. Example: human beta-globin vs. plant leghemoglobin. Analysts can begin to build a common profile for all the personalities and organizations required for WMD development by comparing the timelines and organizational charts built by MDA for many different WMD programs. Critical skills sets, organizational relationships, and proliferation path-

> ways can be identified in this way so that every new MDA of a different WMD or CBRNE program will become easier as a common WMD MDA model is built for each type of WMD and a range of different strategies within that model emerges by analysis of multiple programs.

Biologists now exploit the power of homology searching by using a few simple bioinformatics tools to deduce the function and mechanisms of newly discovered genes by comparison with evidence in DNA, protein, genetic, and other databases—*without having to perform any additional laboratory or field experiments!* Once MDA has been used to profile a few WMD programs, using similar homology searching methods can recall more evidence from the current databases without having to perform new field collection. If analysts concentrate on using systematic MDA-assisted hypothesis testing to build better theories and assessments against a worldwide baseline of WMD programs, not only will our understanding of individual programs greatly improve, but an understanding of WMD proliferation mechanisms will inevitably emerge.

Computers Don't Think, People Think—New Thinking Tools for the Information Age

> A system is defined as a set of different elements so connected or related as to perform a unique function not performable by the elements alone.[61]
>
> Annette Krygiel

Systems, like their biological counterparts, are defined by what they DO, not what they ARE. The "database problem" is not a problem with databases at all. Rather, the problem is to build a new system of people and information technology (IT) systems by which the analysts can, in fact, find Novel Intelligence in Massive Data and can, in fact, provide strategic warning. The new system will be composed of people and computers whereby the computers and the databases they contain will be tools for the analysts to use to become smarter.

The problem with the "database" problem is in first realizing that there are at least four different kinds of databases. Each corresponds to the datasets that researchers already use in hypothesis testing (data repository, data collection, evidence file, and assessment outline) and each is distinct in its format and usage. And it is very important to keep clear the distinction between databases and the datasets they contain. Lessons learned from MDA projects on WMD programs

[61] Krygiel, 32.

indicate that the same data "nugget" can reside in each dataset contained in each database, BUT there is different analytical worth and value-added dependent on where the "nugget" is found.

Getting the Proper Tools to Do the Job: What New Computing Tools Do We Need?

Although the individual kinds of databases and database tools have been around for many years, a major impediment to strategic analysis and MDA is that current IT systems are not set up for hypothesis testing mainly because when one uses the word "system," by current paradigms, one immediately thinks "IT system" rather than "Human/IT system," which does not account for the multiple human-computer and computer-human interactions required to complete the analytical task of building a strategic assessment.

What Data Mining is Not:

- A particular software product or mathematical program
- Just for statisticians
- Turn-key

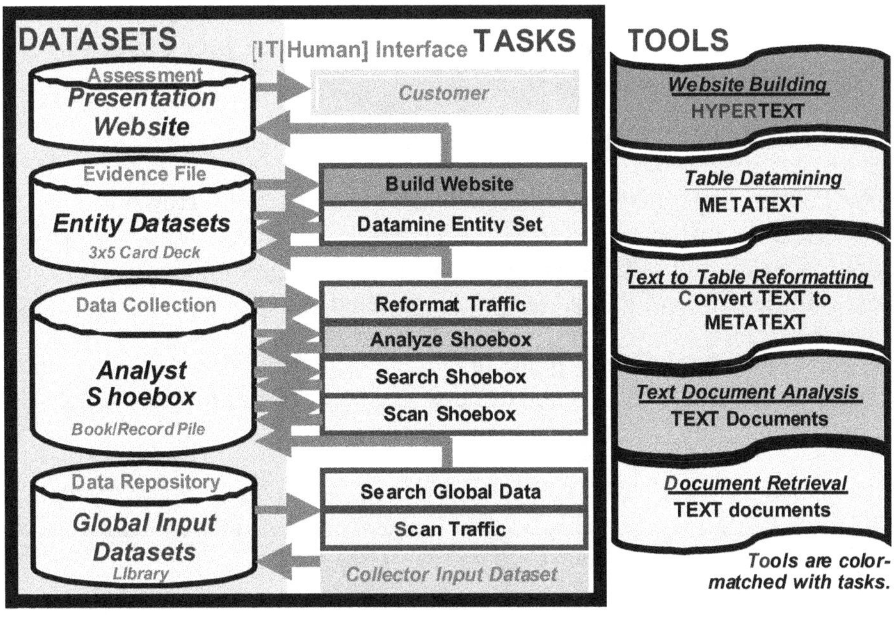

- ❑ Human intervention needed to verify model integrity — "Does it make sense?"
- ❑ Multiple iterations to find good models

- A silver bullet
  - ❑ Data are not informative in and of themselves[62]

We can illustrate the difficulties in the current IC data-handling systems by following the steps an all-source analyst performs in converting data to assessment using the Hypothesis Testing Cycle. At each database (DB) step, there is an input of data which then comprise the particular dataset in that DB, a processing step in which the DB tools perform specific tasks as specified by the analyst, and an output step in which new processed data is presented to the analyst. At each output step, the analyst performs the research tasks in hypothesis testing as outlined above and inputs the processed data into the next DB in much the same way he or she formerly used the library, books, and 3x5 card files. [Several MDA projects have been accomplished using MS Word and PowerPoint as data-manipulation tools because current IC IT systems are unsatisfactory for MDA, mainly due to limitations in IT-human interfaces and data movement among database types. Specific comments on current IC limitations are noted below in brackets.]

Data input to the analytical process is by way of GLOBAL databases (DBs) which are the libraries of the IC: SIGINT from NSA, HUMINT from CIA, Open Source from Foreign Broadcast Information Service (FBIS), and summaries of IMINT data from NIMA. These data represent published messages from the collection agencies and are loaded in a standard TEXT format with a few meta-tags for identification (but not analysis).

(1) GLOBAL DB (Library) = TEXT storage of published records.

Input = Published records from Collectors at CIA, NSA, FBIS, NIMA (text not images).
Processing = Filtering of DBs according to analyst-written Profile.
Output = Presentation of filtered records to the analyst.

As was done with the books in the library, the analyst then scans the presented records from the GLOBAL DB and decides whether records are relevant/not relevant to task.

The analyst then RETRIEVES relevant records and redirects them to the next TEXT storage. In the past, every analyst had a "shoebox" that contained all the

[62] Abbott.

task-relevant documents in whatever format they were retrieved: books, articles, paper copies of intelligence reports. Hypothesis testing is built on doing key experiments based on assumptions of the hypothesis; as alternative hypotheses are tested, discarded, and reconsidered, the researcher needs a place to store and recall the experimental result—the "lab notebook." Since the all-source analyst works with experiments done by others, that is with data input by collectors, this "shoebox" represents the analyst notebook of relevant documents for future reference. This "shoebox" has huge value-added in that the analyst has looked at the document and assessed that the material contained within the document is relevant to the assessments he or she needs to make. [One of the major reasons most IC analysts are prone to stay with their paper copies or MS Word electronic shoeboxes is that no current IT systems have any reasonable methods for building electronic shoeboxes from heterogeneous data. This kind of DB currently does not exist in useable format; Pathfinder on JIVA at DIA is slated to serve this purpose, but available options for data-entry of relevant records by analysts remain too cumbersome to be of any use. A major goal in any IT system used for hypothesis testing or MDA is to be able to build an electronic "shoebox" rapidly and easily.]

(2) DATA COLLECTION/SHOEBOX DB = TEXT storage of task-relevant records.

Input = (1) First-pass analyst input of relevant records.
(2) Feedback input through direct analyst query of or setup to data mining tool.
Processing = TEXT data mining (such as Pathfinder and text-mining analytical tools).
Output = Presentation of filtered or data-mined records to all-source analysts.

Analysts read the presented records from the SHOEBOX DB and:

- Analyze: Analyst evaluates data recalled from SHOEBOX DB by QUERY or by SHOEBOX DB TEXT data mining tool.
- Reformat: Analyst reformats important records into METATEXT for entry into ENTITY DB. These are used in build facility, organization, and project profiles, and personnel biographies.

The data prep is most difficult to characterize.[63]

(3) ENTITY DB (Evidence File) = METATEXT storage of filtered/analyzed records.

---

[63] Abbott.

Input = (1) Analyst Input of METATEXT records: (a) reformatted from SHOE-BOX DB by analyst, or (b) input from already METATAGGED DBs (such as the PubMed online biomedical DB).

(2) Analyst feedback to adjust visual or network displays.

Processing = (1) METATEXT data mining (with data mining tools for tabular data).

(2) MDA Chart presentation (such as by Analyst Notebook)

Output = Presentation of: (1) text or visual displays of data mining
(2) MDA chart displays (with hyperlinks to DATA
COLLECTION DB for original report with highlighted markups).

Analysts view the presented graphs, networks, and the like from the ENTITY DB and:

- Analyze: Analyst evaluates data outputs provided by (1) METATEXT data mining tools or (2) MDA chart presentations or (3) link analysis directly from documents in the shoebox.
- Marshal Evidence: Analyst builds MDA models using maps, time-lines, and organization charts, and builds HYPERTEXT documents for input to PRESENTATION DB.

[Note that since this is all-source analysis at this point, collection analysts at NSA, NIMA, and FBIS should ideally not be expected to do this level of analysis; however, since current collaboration tools are not adequate, the collection analysts must do this to be able to perform the SIGINT, IMINT, or OSINT collection task properly].

[The ENTITY DB will potentially prove to be the most valuable analytical DB in the future, but currently constitutes a huge gap in the IC's repertoire of IT tools. A shared ENTITY DB would be the equivalent of a shared electronic 3x5 card deck. Imagine if a historian were writing a new book on the Civil War and, instead of having just the library for references, could have access to an electronic version of the 3x5 card note decks of Bruce Catton and a dozen other Civil War historians, complete with original references on each. The value added would be immense, not only in tracing hypotheses supported by Catton's books but also in testing hypotheses he may have had and discarded (but kept the cards for future reference) and in testing completely new hypotheses not covered in the linear threads reported in the narratives of his books. However, as Catton's 3x5 card deck might have actually been a pile of highlighted copies of documents and handwritten records, the cost of transferring these documents to electronic format would be enormous. The IC has many senior analysts approaching retirement age who are the "Bruce Catton's" of the IC. Building an ENTITY DB based on the "shoeboxes" of all the retiring IC analysts will certainly be a huge expense, but if it is not done, all the assembled knowledge accumulated by those analysts in using their "shoeboxes" as datasets for hypothesis testing will be lost. Potentially, it could take a "curator" several months to transcribe the "shoebox" of a single retiring analyst into a new electronic SHOEBOX DB and ENTITY DB. However, considering that "smart" bombs are only as smart as the analyst providing the targeting, if the shoebox reformatting of a single analyst cost about $75,000, it need only account for improving the analysis of the next generation analyst well enough to turn a single smart bomb miss into a hit to pay for itself.]

(4) PRESENTATION DB = HYPERTEXT storage of analyzed records.

Input = Analyst input of:

(1) HYPERTEXT maps, timelines, and organization charts (which contain links to ENTITY DB "3x5 cards" and highlighted reports in DATA COLLECTION DB) and;

(2) associated facility, organization, and project profiles, and personnel biographies.
Processing = Website setup for viewing on Intelink (such as the Athena WMD site)
Output = Presentation to policymakers and warfighters either as briefs or as Websites in the PRESENTATION DB.

The challenge for IC analysis and for community resource managers for the 21st Century is to be able to build IT tools that can support hypothesis testing and multidimensional analysis and to make this multidimensional, multi-agency process work in a collaborative environment.

Chapter 11

MODELING OURSELVES

How can we reorient our intelligence process to empower analysts to think strategically? Step 3 in building Warning Analysis for the Information Age is to "reorient the arrows" within the IC—both the information flow and leadership interactions—to provide mechanisms built on Information-Age thinking and thereby be as close to a network as possible. The key to doing this will be to *empower the analyst* to build a new Orientation based on the *hyperword.* [64]

From Looking Outward to Looking Inward

//

ILLUMINATION

- The previous discussion assumes interaction with both the *external* and *internal* environment. Now, let us assume, for whatever reason or combination of circumstances, that we design a command and control system that hinders interaction with the *external* environment. This implies a focus inward, rather than outward.
- Picking up from this idea, we observe from Darwin that:
  - ❑ The environment selects.
  - ❑ Ability or inability to interact and adapt to exigencies of environment select one *in* or *out*.
- Furthermore, according to the Godel Proof, the Heisenberg Uncertainty Principle, and the Second Law of Thermodynamics:
  - ❑ One cannot determine the character or nature of a system within itself.
  - ❑ Moreover, attempts to do so lead to confusion and disorder. Why? Because in the "real world" the environment intrudes (my view).
- Now, by applying the ideas of Darwin, the Second Law, Heisenberg, and Godel to Clausewitz one can see that:

  He who can generate many non-cooperative centers of gravity magnifies friction. Why? Many non-cooperative centers of gravity within a system restrict interaction and adaptability of system with its surroundings, thereby leading to a focus inward (i.e., within itself),

---

[64] The advent of HTML and the ability to hyperlink related ideas and story threads is beginning to change the way we write. I will refer to this new method of writing, which transcends the printed word, as the hyperword.

which in turn generates confusion and disorder, which impedes vigorous or directed activity, hence, by definition, magnifies friction or entropy.[65]

//

Modeling Ourselves

Even with Information-Age methods to model the adversary and tools to implement those models, we still cannot truly put all the pieces together unless we have built an organization to integrate those methods and tools in a coherent manner. But how? Again Col Boyd provides guidance both in what he says and in what he implies. His model for the adversary indicates that our aim should be to "generate many non-cooperative centers of gravity" in the adversary which will foster our ability to be able to think inside his OODA Cycle. Implicit in this message is that we must be able to generate many cooperative centers of gravity within our own organization. Therefore, we need not only to look outward to build better ways to understand the adversary but also to look inward to understand ourselves to build a better IC.

As organizations evolve from loose confederations to integrated systems of systems, the components of the organization redefine their roles—going from working in parallel to working as an integrated team. The increasing demands of the Information Age for quality intelligence and warning analysis requires that the Intelligence Community clearly reorient the roles of its component agencies to do the most with its most scarce asset—its analysts.

> ...various alternative hypotheses may not be given adequate consideration, or even sometimes considered at all, and no systematic effort is made to insure that some group really goes through all the evidence and considers the various alternative explanations in exhaustive detail.
>
> One reason for this, which we have noted before, is that in crises, or budding crisis situations, there is likely to be an overwhelming quantity of information, the mere scanning and preliminary processing of which is consuming most of the analyst's time. There are simply insufficient resources to cope with all the information in any manner, let alone go through a time-consuming process of evaluating each item of information against several hypotheses.[66]

---

[65] Col Boyd.

[66] Grabo, 49.

When young children play soccer, they usually play "clusterball" where virtually all the players are in a tight group trying to kick the ball and only the goalies and a few stray players picking flowers are found elsewhere. As the IC enters the Information Age and data come in at an enormous rate, the IC also appears to be constantly playing "clusterball." The IC is sized to handle a single crisis in a single nation. When there is no apparent crisis, the assets are spread everywhere at a level to handle the pace of current intelligence and maybe a bit of warning. When a crisis comes, most of the assets move to the crisis, and: (1) since there was little warning intelligence being done on the crisis area, the team attempts to do catch-up on the warning that should have been ongoing in that area, and (2) everywhere outside the crisis situation is then so understaffed that partial current intelligence is being done and no warning at all. Should a crisis arise in a new area, the cycle repeats but with less warning and context than before because the normal complement of analysts on the new crisis area is less by having been pulled off to the old crisis area. As the IC moves from crisis to crisis, the ability to do warning becomes less and less. But somehow we must be able to get past this if we are ever going to provide strategic warning.

Furthermore, analysts have virtually no time to analyze information on threats involving other than war or terrorist attack. Threats such as economic, technical, or political infrastructure remain unassessed. As we have seen, strategic analysis requires integration of knowledge about the adversary's infrastructure including logistics, politics, and technical issues.

> It is almost impossible to give too much stress to the importance of the most meticulous and exhaustive examination of all available information prior to reaching warning judgments. It is erroneous to presume that all research will automatically be accomplished in a crisis or budding crisis situations, or that the organization and distribution of work within the office or offices involved is necessarily adequate for the purpose... The inadequate examination of available evidence has been a contributing cause to nearly every warning failure and in some cases should probably be considered the major cause of failure.[67]

Strategic warning must be proactive, actively building, testing, discarding and rebuilding hypotheses. The ultimate goal of strategic analysis is to be able to provide actionable guidance early enough so that the situation can be changed before it becomes a crisis.

---

[67] Grabo, 163.

The mere fact that a "crisis action team" needs to be formed is an indicator of the failure of strategic warning. For if there were prior indication of the impending "crisis," it would have been evident that such a team was needed *prior* to the crisis.

As a former submariner, I must contend that the true indicator that strategic warning and deterrence is working properly goes even a step further... The best indicator of an IC that is providing satisfactory strategic warning is that *nothing happens.* Every submariner knows that the only way a submariner will ever make the news or show up on CNN is if he *fails* at his job. In peacetime, submariners are invisible unless they collide with someone or run aground. Even in wartime, submarine successes are proactive—behind enemy lines where only the result may be important, and with few or no BDA photos. In fact, every submariner (especially those responsible for nuclear weapons) understands that the mere fact that a war starts means that he has *failed* in his primary mission—deterring a war.

Similarly, I contend that in the Age of WMD and terrorism, the standard for the Intelligence Community must be to provide strategic warning such that *NOTHING HAPPENS.* From the standpoint of the IC:

- The only acceptable WMD attack is one that never happens.
- The only acceptable Weapon of Mass Destruction is one that is never built.
- The only acceptable terrorist attack is one that never happens.
- The only acceptable terrorist WMD program is one that is never built.

MDA can provide a tool for strategic warning *only* if there are enough assets and time to build the 6-D MDA model of the adversary and to use that model for actionable intelligence production.

> It is possible to examine all available information and still not to understand its significance in relation to intentions... Some relevant information is likely to come from highly classified sources—such as covertly acquired military documents—and therefore has been extremely restricted in distribution. Some developments are likely to be highly technical and understood by very few persons, but their interpretation and integration with other information can be critical to an understanding of what is really happening... In warning episodes, the need of the community for expert assistance in a whole range of military subjects—and to a lesser extent, political—skyrockets.[68]

---

[68] Grabo, 164.

To make matters worse, even the collected data and the 6-D model may be uninterpretable if the data are outside the analyst's area of expertise. Therefore, to work at all, MDA must be done by a team of analysts.

> A system of systems is a set of different systems so connected or related as to produce results unachievable by the individual systems alone.[69]

Cooperation is the answer, but how can we build cooperation in the IC?

Another major stumbling block to Information-Age analysis is the mismatch of analytical methods and organizations with IT tools. The most prevalent failure mode has been the introduction of next-generation tools into current organizations using current intelligence methods. This "drive-by" dumping of new technologies onto analysts with no thought about how they interface with analytical methods and organizations results in frustrated analysts who now have "new" tools that they are expected to use that do not work and frustrated managers who invested in new tools that they cannot sell to their subordinates. A few simple examples of this kind mismanagement:

- *Buying "one-size-fits-all" business applications under the COTS program and implementing them with no thought to how they apply in the IC.* For example, in MS Word when an analyst types "(C)" to denote a Confidential paragraph, the computer changes that "(C)" into "(c)" for copyright; when the analyst then hits "Enter" at the end of that paragraph, the computer may also put a "(D)" to "help" the "outline" expected to continue in the new paragraph. Very few programs are ever customized to fit analysts' needs prior to appearing on their computer desktops.
- *No thoughts of consolidating individual proprietary software into a single system.* Analysts cannot understand why there is computer technology to identify terrorists by TV in airports, but that the computer system they are using requires as many as 14 separate passwords just to do their job. Why cannot a system be implemented that recognizes only a single password for a single analyst?
- *No thoughts of interfaces between software on the system.* Currently at DIA the "Global Database" is called WebSafe and the best tool that analysts could use for a "Shoebox" is Pathfinder; however, the only way to transfer "relevant" items identified in WebSafe to Pathfinder for further analysis is for the analyst to E-mail the individual messages

[69] Krygiel, 33.

> to himself then write his own macro tool to enter them in Pathfinder. Without an easy-to-use interface between the agency's "retrieval" tool and its "analysis" tool, very few analysts use Pathfinder, but there is no management chain to require the two independent contractors to link their tools.

Unless new methodologies are already in place and the organizations are reoriented to use them, tools development will be as useful to an analyst as a new DVD player would be to a music lover who owns several hundred records and cassettes. Music lovers don't care what the format is, so long as they can listen to the music. Analysts don't care what the format is, so long as they can recall and read the relevant documents in their shoebox. However, to implement such a system requires cooperation between analytical organizations and the IT organizations and contractors that support them.

> The Digital Production System (DPS) was a 10-year development by the Defense Mapping Agency (DMA) to deliver an end-to-end digital processing pipeline for production of mapping, charting, and geodesy products. [p. 50]... For the DPS program management, full realization of the level of resources required and the extent of expertise needed to make a SOS [System of Systems] out of a set of individual systems did not come until the beginning of the IOC integration activities. [p. 110]... "We had some idea of how many (people) were needed and did in fact program for them, but what was unknown was the amount of information people had to absorb and understand."[70]

Again, cooperation is the answer, but how can we build cooperation in the IC?

Orienting Is More Important Than Deciding

//

COMMENT

Up to this point we have shown orientation as being a critical element in command and control—implying that without orientation there is no command and control worthy of the name.

[70] Krygiel, 111.

VERY NICE

But, simply stated, what does this comment and everything else we've discussed so far tell us about command and control?

//

ILLUMINATION

- ❑ The process of observation-orientation-decision-action represents what takes place during the command and control process—which means that the O-O-D-A loop can be thought of as being the C&C loop.
- ❑ The second O, orientation—as the repository of our genetic heritage, cultural tradition, and previous experiences—is the most important part of the O-O-D-A loop since it shapes the way we observe, the way we decide, the way we act.

IMPLICATION

- ❑ Operating inside adversary's O-O-D-A loop means the same thing as operating inside adversary's C&C loop.[71]

//

I suggest that we can build organizations for the Information Age based on Col Boyd's assessment, but we must remember that Col Boyd was modeling the military and that the military is only a part of the national organization. We should consider that what are strategic decisions from the standpoint of the military are tactical decisions from the national standpoint. Therefore, one must realize that the national OODA loop transcends just military organizations and decisions and includes civilian ones as well. And in the national OODA loop, the IC is entrusted with the intelligence half (observing and orienting) while the IC consumers are entrusted with the operations half (deciding and acting).

Therefore, to build a national OODA Cycle for the Information Age we need to remember:

- The intelligence (OO) half of the national OODA Cycle is the responsibility of the IC.
- The IC spends billions of dollars on researching and improving the Observe-Orient part of the cycle but virtually all the dollars go into the "Observe" category on new collection methods and new databases in which to store the collected data.

---

[71]Col Boyd.

- There is "Massive Data" going into the databases around the IC, but only the same Industrial-Age knowledge is coming out of those databases.

Therefore:

- It is the Orientation step in the national OODA Cycle that is broken.
- As Col Boyd has stated, "the second O, orientation—as the repository of our shared hypotheses and models of the world—is the most important part of the OODA loop since it shapes the way we observe, the way, we decide, the way we act."
- The only way to "orient the arrows" rather than merely connect the dots, is to reorient the way the components of the IC interact to Orient—build hypotheses, theories, and knowledge from those databases.

Toward an IC that Can Orient as a Team

Orienting is analysis. Strategic analysis orients the national organization to make plans not only for the current OODA Cycle but also to provide new insights to be able plan two OODA Cycles ahead—one logistics cycle and the following operational cycle.

Strategic analysis requires methods, tools, and organizations. From my work on a variety of successful and unsuccessful attempts by DIA and the IC to build intelligence on Information Technology, I have noted that the interdependence of methods, tools, and organizations has led to a vicious cycle that has derailed virtually every effort to move intelligence analysis into the Information Age. New analytical methods require new computer tools that require new organizational interrelationships that require new analytical methods...

The single most important insight into making MDA a reality (as demonstrated by the accompanying case studies) was the realization that a new methodology *can* be implemented with current tools and organizations *if* the analysts involved desire (or are allowed) to take the time to build new methods by reorienting: from collection-driven analysis to hypothesis-driven analysis using MDA; from software-driven tools usage to methodology-driven tools usage; and from organization-driven teamwork to hypothesis-driven teamwork.

From Collection-Driven Analysis to Hypothesis-Driven Analysis

Step 1 toward warning analysis for the Information Age is methodology—modeling the adversary. Multidimensional analysis is a first step in that direction.

From Software-Driven Tools Usage to Methodology-Driven Tools Usage

Step 2 toward warning analysis for the Information Age is tools—modeling how we model. Given a methodology, one can build tools to support it. Surprisingly, current tools available on almost any computer such a MS Word and PowerPoint can support hypothesis testing and MDA—as long as the analysts involved know what they desire to do. While most IT experts don't consider either one "state-of-the-art," when compared with Newtonian data management tools—pencil and paper and real paper 3x5 cards—MS Word and Powerpoint are amazing tools. Hypothesis testing requires building a "shoebox" and a "3x5 card deck," which depend only on having the capability to cut-and-paste and to hyperlink. MDA requires drawing charts (maps, timelines, and organizational charts), which depend only on having capability to cut-and-paste and to draw block diagrams and annotate imported maps. Therefore, implementing MDA and hypothesis testing *is* doable with current tools. Certainly it will become easier as methodology-driven tools become available, but we need not wait until then to start the process.

> The collector in the field who elects to forward, or not to forward, some fragment of information to his home office is making a judgment. The current analyst, who decides to write up a given piece of information, or not to do so, is making a judgment about it. The manner in which he writes up, the emphasis he gives to this or that aspect of it, constitutes another judgment. The items that his immediate supervisor selects to include in a briefing for the senior officials of his agency or department are the result of another judgment.[72]

From Organization-Driven Teamwork to Hypothesis-Driven Teamwork

Step 3 in building Warning Analysis for the Information Age is to "reorient the arrows" within the IC—modeling ourselves. Lessons learned from two IC-wide BW analysis projects have indicated how the IC-organizations need to be reoriented—but not necessarily reorganized—to implement MDA on an IC-wide scale thereby preventing the "confusion and disorder" foreseen by Col Boyd. Today's IC is collection-driven; collectors provide raw data which are analyzed by collection analysts (DO, NSA, FBIS, and NIMA) and those data enter the system as intelligence reporting. The repository for reporting (each individual agency's version of a "Global Database") is then exploited individually by the entire IC. In

[72] Grabo, 133.

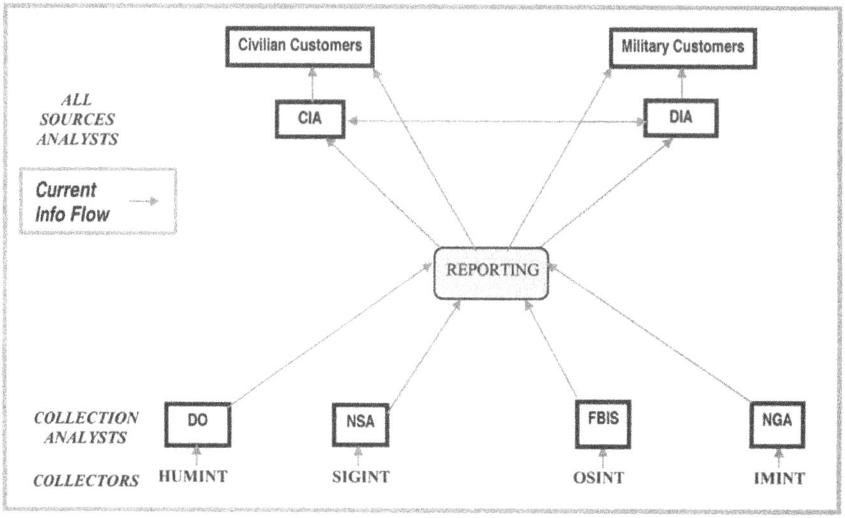

essence the collection agencies (DO, NSA, FBIS, and NIMA) perform the Observation step in the national OODA cycle, the IC customers perform the Decision step, but the Orientation step is done catch-as-catch-can independently by everyone across the community from collectors to analysts to decisionmakers.

How is it that Orientation—the most important step in the OODA cycle—is the one with the least support?

The Next RMA will be a Revolution in Orientation

A re-examination of the OODA Cycle itself indicates that the current national version of the cycle is built on Newtonian thinking. The Newtonian paradigm was a revolution in the *physical* sciences—that is, in the way we can model and understand the *physical* world. Accordingly, the Industrial Age revolutionized the way we can observe and measure the physical world, beginning with the telescope and microscope and moving onward to their lineal descendants such as the satellite camera and signal interception receivers, and also the way we can act to control the physical world beginning with the steam engine to propel a ship and a cotton gin for mass production and moving onward to their lineal descendants, the mass-produced cruise missile and smart bomb.

The Newtonian revolution enabled the Observation and Action steps in the OODA Cycle. Therefore, current projections that the next-generation military will be based on significantly improved Observation through sensor

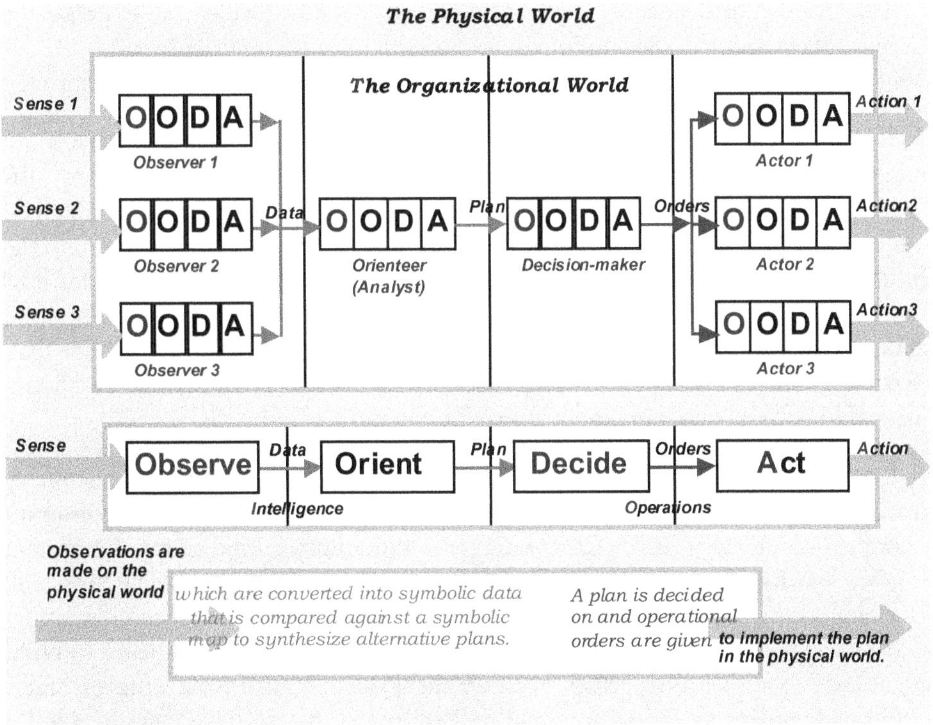

technology and Action through more advanced delivery devices are based on Newtonian thinking.

The major paradigm shift from Agricultural-Age to Industrial-Age thinking in land warfare came during the Civil War. Early in the war, when Lee was fighting Hancock and Meade, he was able to prevail due to their Agricultural-Age thinking. Ulysses Grant brought land warfare into the Industrial Age with maneuver based on the railroad, steamship, and telegraph plus "shock and awe" based on mass-produced firepower in a drafted citizen army. While current weapons are faster and more powerful with longer ranges, the doctrine for their employment is not very different from Grant's strategy. For example, Sherman marched to the Sea for much the same reason as Rumsfeld marched to Baghdad, and the idea of using "precision" munitions was very much the same at the Petersburg Crater (where a tunnel was used to place explosives under Confederate positions) and in the precision attacks on Saddam Hussein's bunkers. This continuity in Industrial-Age warfare is mainly due to the lack of changes in the Orientation and Decision steps in the national OODA cycle. The use of intelligence reporting in Orienting is not very different in today's Pentagon than it was in Grant's tent; therefore, one should not expect today's Decisionmaking to be any more complex or directed than Grant's was.

The Orientation-Decision steps in the national OODA Cycle have not changed because they occur in the *organizational* world—not the *physical* world. That is why they will require Quantum thinking—not Newtonian thinking—to improve.

Common wisdom suggests that Revolutions in Military Affairs (RMAs) are intertwined with technological advances. However, the current RMA seems different, especially when one reflects on the trend that all the RMAs that changed our ability to Observe and to Act, since U.S. Grant brought land warfare into the Industrial Age, appear to be sensor and/or weapons-related. I suggest that the current revolution is a different kind that is more akin to the revolutions brought about by the invention of the written word and of the printed word. Rather than expecting this revolution to change the way we Observe and Act, we should instead look to its changing the way we Orient and Decide.

Communities are built on communication, and one can parallel the customary revolutions that follow the evolution of technology—which change the Observation and Action steps in the OODA Cycle—with another kind of revolution that follows the evolution of communication—which changes the Orientation and Decision steps. Humankind evolved organizations using language, beginning with the spoken word. A society based on the spoken word could begin to build organizations as large as tribes because the Decisionmaker, the king or chief, could pass orders as far as he could yell or one of his followers could retell a remembered order and also he could observe as far as his followers could yell or retell a remembered observation.

> The second O, orientation—as the repository of our genetic heritage, cultural tradition, and previous experiences—is the most important part of the O-O-D-A loop since it shapes the way we observe, the way, we decide, the way we act.[73]

But the tribe would flourish only if the Orienter could pass remembered experiences on to the next generation—where the best hunting grounds were, how one could tell by the stars or length of day when to start moving south for winter or even how to tell which way South is. Societies began to have two kinds of leaders—a Soldier or Strongman who was responsible for organizational Decisions and a Teacher or Wiseman who was responsible for organizational Orientation. Advances that empowered control over the physical world also empowered the Strongman—fire, tools, domesticated animals, and crop cultivation. Societies grew larger but were still limited by the oral tradition; the cultural tradition or organizational world model was limited by what could be remembered—by a

---

[73] Col Boyd.

messenger to and from the edges of the tribal lands or by the Wiseman and his protégés to the next generation.

With the invention of the written word—again a technological advance—tribes could become Empires as the Babylonians, Egyptians, Chinese, and Romans all showed. The Strongman could receive observations written in remote parts of the empire and send orders to the ends of the empire written as royal decrees. But the written word diffused the power of the Wiseman to a class of priests and teachers who would maintain the organizational Orientation as written texts in temples and libraries. But empires could flourish because societies could remember—and orient—over generations through the written word.

With the invention of the printed word, the role of the Strongman did not change very much but the power of the Wiseman was markedly affected. One of the financial backers of Gutenberg's project to build a printing press was a Cardinal who believed that when everyone could read from an identical Bible, the power of the Pope would increase. But instead, the power of the Wiseman was again diffused down another level—to the bourgeoisie—and to three differing kinds of Wisemen who were the Orienteers for society. Clergy like Martin Luther and Calvin could print their own version of the Bible and begin the Protestant revolution; scientists like Newton and Leibnitz could trade ideas by writing books that all could read and begin a scientific revolution; and political activists like Thomas Paine and John Adams could spread new ideas by printing pamphlets and newspapers. It was this orientation revolution that provided a new cultural tradition shared by the printed word that then served as the basis for the coming Industrial Age.

I suggest that the invention of electronic communications and the resulting development of the hyperword is the technology that portends to start a new revolution as large as those brought about by the spoken word, written word, and printed word. And as was seen in those revolutions, I expect that the core of that revolution will center on Orientation—how we will build a new kind of shared cultural tradition built on the hyperword.

Therefore, the key to improving the all-important Orientation step is in reorienting current organizations. And based on the previous orientation revolutions, I expect that the effect of the hyperword will be to empower the Wiseman rather than the Strongman and diffuse that power down yet another level. In short, I suggest that the key to the Information Age will be to *empower the analyst*—by connecting or networking him or her with evidence to test hypotheses, with other analysts to test hypotheses cooperatively, with collectors to bring new data to support or refute those hypotheses, and with customers to provide strategic and well as tactical warning.

Empowering the Analyst

As shown above, information flow in the current IC is streamlined from collector to customer, from observer to decisionmaker. Its hierarchical nature is exactly what one would expect for an organization in an unchanging environment like the Cold War where all agreed on a common world model (orientation) of a two-player-zero-sum-game. But in a time of change, a network is much smarter in building a new world model (orientation). In a new orientation revolution that is being built on the hyperword, one would also expect that a new kind of Wisemen would be critical and a new kind of medium of communication will emerge—much like the written manuscript or printed book. Lessons learned from two recent team experiments in BW analysis suggest the first steps toward the new way of national Orientation will depend on empowering analysts to build a web-based "hyperbook." And I suggest that the first "hyperbooks' will be websites that can present a 6-D hierarchical MDA model of the world.

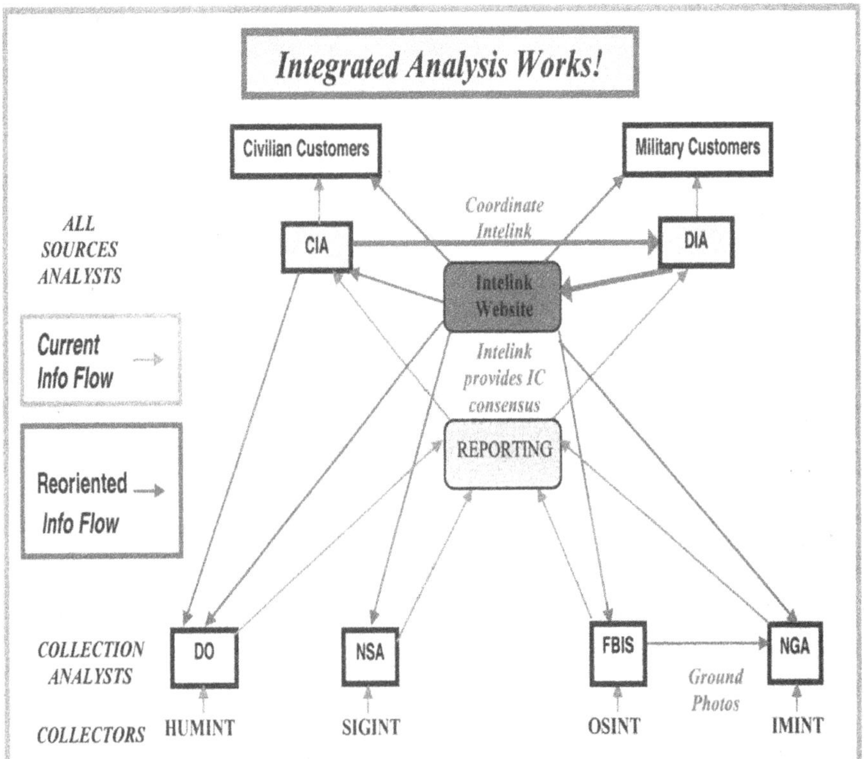

The organization of the IC in this new worldview is the same, only the orientation is different and, therefore, lines of communication that enable the organizations to work as an "orientation team" are also different.

Again, it is important to note that the Orientation step is the one that needs fixing and that Cynthia Grabo's "strategic warning," Col Boyd's "orientation," and my "models" are different views on the same important concept—an organization can only make decisions that are as smart as the common worldview that is shared by the "Wisemen" of that organization.

How will this new kind of Orientation for the national OODA Cycle occur?

In the reoriented IC, intelligence will be hypothesis-driven (employing Top-Down models) rather than collection-driven (employing Bottom-Up models). It will also be proactive (building a worldview by modeling wherever the hypothesis testing Research Cycle leads) rather than reactive (building a worldview in response to customer tasking).

The key is providing the all-source analysts the time and tools they need to build an MDA model of the target nations or organizations. This common model is then shared upward and downward in the old information flow pattern but with added links. The common MDA model is posted as a website on Intelink based on the 6-D hierarchical MDA model.

Experiments in posting an MDA WMD model on Intelink empowered everyone across the IC who was part of the project. But this depended on the all-source analysts to provide guidance and orientation:

- Since DIA took responsibility for posting the common model on an Intelink site, CIA and DIA analysts needed to work more closely. DIA needed to ensure that the model posted represented community consensus (or noted community disagreements where needed), and CIA needed to monitor the site to again ensure that the site reflected common assessments but also to ensure that they reflected reporting above the classification of the site (since such sensitive reporting is usually in the realm of the CIA analyst).
- The first level of intelligence posted was strategic analysis that provided quick and easy availability of key assessments to both civilian and military policymakers.
- The second level of intelligence posted contained detailed descriptions from MDA that included organizational histories and resumes of key WMD personnel including those that were assessed to be only dual-use and not currently a part of the WMD program. This level of information sharing helped provide

detailed feedback to the collection analysts and collectors for much improved collection targeting.

- The most surprising result was that after about a year into the experiment, the all-source analysts began getting *fewer* questions and *fewer* taskers from customers even though MDA concentrates on building models rather than directly addressing customer concerns. The proactive history and context of the WMD program is so much more detailed using MDA that new information is much easier to orient within that larger context. Thus, questions from customers could usually be answered by providing the URL to the appropriate Intelink posting. Thereafter, the number of questions dropped dramatically, but the ones that came in were much more informed because those customers already had a broader context from what was posted on Intelink.

The two-year IC-wide MDA effort has led to the identification of four new biotechnology facilities and localization of four known BW facilities in the target country as well as facilitating building an organizational chart and list of key players in that country's BW program.

I suggest that the current IC organization is adequate to bring intelligence into the Information Age. By reorienting the lines of communication from hierarchical (taskers flowing down and reporting flowing up) to network-like, the IC *can* provide strategic warning in a world of WMD and terrorism. The key to that is concentrating on fixing the Orientation Step in the national OODA Cycle. And the key to that is empowering the collection analyst to become the "Wiseman" for Observing and empowering the all-source analyst to become the "Wiseman" for Orienting.

Chapter 12

GETTING THERE FROM HERE

We have the methods, tools, and organizations to reorient the IC toward Information-Age intelligence that can build strategic warning. Can we find the leadership to get there?

How can we reorient our intelligence process to think strategically given that we have organizations that are designed to act tactically?

From Industrial-Age Reacting to Information-Age Thinking

As intelligence collection becomes more sophisticated, voluminous and expensive, and devices multiply for the rapid reporting and community-wide exchange and display of the latest information, we must take care that we do not lose sight of what warning really is: the considered judgment of the finest analytic minds available, based on an exhaustive and objective review of all available indications, which is conveyed to the policy official in sufficiently convincing language that he is persuaded of its validity and takes appropriate action to protect the national interest.[74]

//

NOW WE CAN SEE BY GOING BACK TO THE BEGINNING

The Strategic Game
is one of
Interaction and Isolation

A game in which we must be able to diminish adversary's ability to communicate or interact with his environment while sustaining or improving ours.[75]

//

In the new age of WMD and terrorism, the IC is faced with an unprecedented challenge: How can it provide strategic warning in a world of WMD where a massive attack from half-a-world away can occur minutes from now? How can it provide tactical warning in a world of terrorism where adversaries who looked

[74] Grabo, 169.
[75] Col Boyd.

peaceful minutes ago can attack inside the U.S. minutes from now? The first step to meeting this challenge comes from understanding the difference between current intelligence, tactical warning, and strategic warning:

- **Current Intelligence** — matching recently collected intelligence against warning indicators to predict the next actions of the adversary.
- **Tactical Warning** — warning of potential actions by an adversary to which a response can be mounted with current resources.
- **Strategic Warning** — warning of potential actions by an adversary to which a response will require significant reallocations of resources.

Tactical warning is possible from knowledge of what the adversary is doing *now*—if one can build knowledge of not only the weapons he has available but also the people and organizations that will employ them. If we can know what they currently have, we can decide what we can do in response with what we currently have. But for strategic warning, we need first to get inside his head and secondly to get inside our own heads. The strategic OODA Cycle begins with a plan to reallocate resources to build a new infrastructure then moves on to a plan to use that new infrastructure.

Strategic warning requires understanding the adversary's strategic plan and that plan must begin with a decision to build a new infrastructure. To employ WMD one first needs to build them. To employ CBRNE (chemical, biological, radiological, nuclear and explosive) weapons in a terrorist attack one first needs to build them. Therefore, the warning analyst needs not only to know the adversary's capabilities, what he can do now, but also his intentions, what he is planning to do.

> If we want to assess an adversary's capabilities, we can do so by "connecting the dots."
>
> If we want to assess an adversary's intentions, we need to "orient the arrows."

BUT, those warning analyses have to be ready *before* the crisis. For if nations or terrorists use WMD to start the crisis, we are already too late.

New Assumptions for Information-Age Intelligence

I have indicated a path toward a reoriented IC that can provide strategic warning in a world of WMD and terrorism. The good news is that getting there *is* possible within a decade given leadership that can transcend Newtonian, Industrial-Age thinking and move to Quantum, Information-Age thinking.

From...	To...
Bigger Faster Technology, Fighting against Technologies, and Instantaneous data leading to instantaneous decisions.	Smarter Thinking, Out-Thinking Decisionmakers, and Projecting the future only by knowing the past. History Matters!

From...	To...
Targeting Objects. It's a bipolar world.	Targeting Individuals. It's a multi-polar world where every nation, organization, and individual has distinct goals and decisionmaking processes to reach those goals.
It's "Us" versus "Them."	It's "Our team" working together.

From...	To...
One size fits all.	It all depends. Context is critical.
Assessment of capabilities built on understanding and identifying things—weapons and the facilities that make them.	Assessment of intent built on understanding people and the organizations, nations, and cultures they built—for it is people who build WMD and become terrorists.

From...	To...
Intelligence that is reactive, collection-driven, and built on current intelligence and tactical warning.	Intelligence that is proactive. hypothesis-drivien, and built on strategic warning.
In tactical thinking, faster is better.	In strategic thinking, smarter is better.

True strategic warning needs to plan ahead not only into the next Decision Cycle but the Decision Cycle beyond that. The object of intelligence—just like the object of science—is to predict the future.

Using those quantum assumptions, I have outlined ways to model the adversary, model how we model, and model ourselves that indicate the first steps to take in our thousand-mile-journey toward an Information-Age IC. We have the required methods and the required tools and technologies. We even have the required organizations, but we need to reorient how intelligence thinks. Again, based on lessons learned from experiments in MDA of WMD programs, the good news is that such a process is possible within a decade should we reorient and apply ourselves to do so.

Chapter 13

TOWARD AN INFORMATION-AGE IC: HOW LONG WILL IT TAKE?

Changing cultures usually requires generations. Can we reorient IC culture from the Newtonian paradigm to a Quantum paradigm in a shorter time than the four generations it took the Navy to go from sail to steam or to go from segregated to integrated?

From Observations Driving Actions to Orientation Driving Decisions

> Warning is an intangible, an abstraction, a theory, a deduction, a perception, a belief. It is the product of reasoning or of logic, a hypothesis whose validity can be neither confirmed nor refuted until it is too late.[76]

> The second O, orientation—as the repository of our genetic heritage, cultural tradition, and previous experiences—is the most important part of the O-O-D-A loop since it shapes the way we observe, the way, we decide, the way we act.[77]

The bad news is that reorienting ourselves will not be easy. Our organizations are set up on an Industrial-Age model that emphasizes Action driven directly by Observation. This is not surprising because thinking logically within the Newtonian paradigm centered on our command of the physical world. But thinking logically in the emerging quantum paradigm centers on our command of the conceptual world. This means that we need an Information-Age model that emphasizes Decisionmaking driven by timely Orientation. The leaders in the Industrial-Age RMAs were "Strongmen" or "Soldiers" who made decisions and acted. The current RMA portends to be an orientation revolution like the one based on the invention of the printed word that predated and drove the Industrial Age. The leaders in that kind of revolution were "Wisemen" or "Teachers" like Martin Luther, Isaac Newton, and Thomas Paine.

---

[76] Grabo, 4.

[77] Col Boyd.

In a stable world hierarchies work best and the "Soldier" leads by emphasis on the physical world—Observation drives Action. In a rapidly changing world networks work best and the "Teacher" leads by emphasis on the cognitive world—Observation drives Orientation. By examining two RMAs of the second kind, we can see that such reorientations of organizational thinking usually take several generations.

We have met the enemy and they are us.
Pogo

Military Technical Revolutions (MTRs), which change the world by changing technologies, can happen rapidly. The early Civil War battles were bloodbaths due to Industrial-age technologies even though the generals were still using Agricultural-Age tactics. RMAs, which change the world by changing how organizations work, happen more slowly. Grant needed to reorganize the way armies work to bring in Industrial-Age strategies. Revolutions in Military Culture (RMCs), which change the way organizations think by changing the way that individuals that comprise them think, by comparison, happen at a glacial pace.

How Long Does It Take to Change a Culture?

> ... a naval captain who fought in the Invincible Armada [1588] would have been more at home in the typical warship of 1840, than the average captain of 1840 would have been in the advanced types of the American Civil War [1861-1865].[78]
>
> CAPT Alfred Thayer Mahan
> *From Sail to Steam*

A problem with paradigm shifts is that those who grew up in the old paradigm have a very difficult time reorienting their own thinking to the new technologies and organizations built on them. This usually means that an MTR can become an RMA in just a few years but an RMC usually takes generations. The revolution of the U.S. Navy going from sail to steam provides an example.

[78] Alfred Thayer Mahan, *From Sail to Steam* (New York: Harper & Brothers, 1907), 3.

Robert Fulton sailed the steamship *Clermont* on the Hudson River in 1807. The ironclads *USS Monitor* and *CSS Virginia* fought in 1862. However, even after successful use of other ironclad steam Monitors throughout the remainder of the war, the U.S. Navy was still very reluctant to give up its sails. The ability to sail on any point of the compass at will—even into the wind or when becalmed—changed the tactical picture, but the technology outstripped the tactics and organizational thinking. This period of history was marked by the days of the "steam sloop"—a true oxymoron. The Navy even replaced the four-bladed screws on many ships with less efficient two-bladed screws, which could be lined up vertically with the keel to increase speed when the ship was under sail.[79]

Steam Sloop USS Galena
(built 1871-1879; wrecked 1891).
(Norfolk Naval Shipyard)

In the Age of Sail officer candidates were trained on-the-job aboard ship. Since they were not either enlisted (who bunked in the foc'sle-forecastle-or bow of the ship) or truly officers (who were berthed in the stern), they were berthed amidships—hence Midshipmen, a name that persists today. Their training was mostly informal, usually by the ship's chaplain, and they learned the ropes quite literally by climbing masts and furling sails. However, technology and scandal changed that. With steamships becoming more prevalent throughout the fleet, there was concern about how to train officers on boilers and screws and all the engineering principles involved, with the debate focusing in the 1830s on whether to open a school to do so. The final blow to shipboard education, however, was an incident on board the *USS Somers* in 1842 in which a Midshipman and two enlisted conspirators were hanged for mutiny. The ship's Captain was cleared of any wrong in the incident, but since the Midshipman was the son of the Secretary of War and nephew of a Navy Captain, the ensuing furor led to the foundation of the U.S. Naval Academy in Annapolis, MD in 1845. Even though the Naval Academy was founded in response to the advent of steamships, the paradigm shift from sail to steam was incomplete until the first Midshipman summer cruise was made on a steam vessel in 1910.[80]

---

79 *Sea Power: A Naval History*, E. B. Potter, ed. (Annapolis, MD: Naval Institute Press, 1981), 117-120, 128, 155-161.

80 *Sea Power: A Naval History*, 112, 163.

Even though Fulton steamed the Clermont up the Hudson River in 1810, the Navy's sail-to-steam MTR did not begin for another generation with the commissioning of the first steamships in the 1830s, the foundation of the Naval Academy in 1845, and the Monitor-Virginia clash in 1862. Even then, the sail-to-steam RMC did not truly begin until CAPT Mahan's book, *The Influence of Seapower on History*, began to reorient the Navy in the 1880s, leading to the true steam Navy with President Roosevelt's Great White Fleet and the first Naval Academy steamship summer cruise after the turn of the century. Thus it took steamship technology almost a century before it became an integral part of Navy culture.[81]

> A new scientific truth does not triumph by convincing its opponents and making them see the light, but rather because its opponents eventually die, and a new generation grows up that is familiar with it.
>
> Max Planck

Why the resistance to change? Why does it take generations for a true RMC? It appears that most people solidify their worldview and way of thinking before they leave school. Whatever they learned in growing up and in formal classes, they later put into practice for the remainder of their careers.

Example two is the segregation-to-integration revolution in the U.S. Navy.[82] President Roosevelt moved to integrate the Navy in 1942, but even then integration only started at the Naval Academy under duress in 1945 with the admission of the first Black Midshipman, Wesley Brown, who graduated from the U.S. Naval Academy in 1948. Even though the color-barrier was supposedly broken, it wasn't until 1969 that the fiftieth Black Midshipman graduated. And even then, by 1999, the Naval Academy could only boast of four Black graduates who had been promoted to Admiral.

Again it took several generations to go from RMA, with Roosevelt's order to integrate, to RMC with a totally integrated Navy. President Truman reiterated the integration goal with an executive order in 1948, establishing a policy of equal treatment and opportunity in the armed forces, but integration at the Academy did not really occur until the 1970s where the number of Black graduates rose from only three in 1971 to over sixty in 1977. Academy graduates from the first on-paper integrated classes in the late 1940s finally became the Navy's senior leadership—the Admirals with about thirty years service—in the mid 1970s. They were the first Naval Officers to spend an entire career with an official policy of integra-

---

[81] *Sea Power: A Naval History*, 162, 174, 192-193.

[82] John W. Bodnar, "How Long Does It Take to Change a Culture? Integration at the U.S. Naval Academy," *Armed Forces and Society* 25, no. 2 (Winter 1999): 286. Cited hereafter as Bodnar.

tion, and it followed that they were the first Naval Officers to truly support and implement that policy. Also, demographics dictated that until 1975 there were virtually no Black officers in the pool of Admiral candidates. The fact that four Black graduates made Admiral by 1999—drawing off the classes of 1948 to 1975 which graduated only 178 Blacks total—is actually a credit for integration in that the probability of an individual Black making Admiral was not very different from that of a white classmate.[83]

One need only do the addition to track the progression of an RMC: changes brought by an MTR in reference year zero will not have proponents comfortable with them in senior leadership until almost year thirty at which point one might expect a change in policy and organization to begin an RMA. But the organization will not "think" in the new paradigm until the students of year thirty themselves become senior leadership.

The sail-to-steam revolution in the Navy took over half-a-century. The Navy went from sail to steam in the 1840s; the first Midshipman "born and raised" on steamships did not make Admiral until the 1870s, including Mahan, who would reorient the Navy to "thinking" steamships, but it was not until the early 1900s that everyone in the Navy was trained by the first-generation steamship Admirals. The progression of the 1845 founding of the Naval Academy to the 1910 Midshipman steamship cruise follows the same pattern: it took Mahan, an 1859 Academy graduate, to reorient his generation before they assumed leadership and became decisionmakers based on a steamship orientation.

The segregation-to-integration revolution in the Navy is also taking half-a-century. Naval Academy graduates who were classmates of Wesley Brown in 1948 "grew up" in a Navy that was always integrated—on paper at least. When they became Admirals in the late 1960s, going from "on paper" integration to true integration was not an issue because the Navy they knew was always integrated. The first truly integrated Academy classes of the mid-1970s are finally assuming senior leadership roles as Admirals as we turn into the new century. Not only is the number of Black Admirals increasing dramatically because of the larger candidate pool of the 1970s but also everyone in today's Navy never knew a time when the Navy wasn't integrated. Thus the reorientation process of segregationist thinking to integrationist thinking is *finally* reaching maturity over half-a-century after Roosevelt's order.

[83] Bodnar.

When Can We Expect to Reorient from Newtonian Thinking to Quantum Thinking?

Just as Multidisciplinary Analysis predicts a lengthy process for an adversary to change its strategic thinking, examining our own reorientations to new strategic paradigms indicates that we are subject to the same cultural and institutional limitations on change. To predict when the RMC will emerge in the wake of the change from Industrial-Age thinking to Information-Age thinking, one again need only do the addition and demography.

IF

You graduated from college Before 1965...	After 1980...
You're more comfortable calculating than computing.	You're more comfortable computing than calculating.
In the last science class you took, you used a slide rule.	In the last science class you took, you used a calculator.
In biology class you cut up dead cats.	In biology class you analyzed DNA.
You live in the world of the printed word.	You live in the world of the hyperword.
Your main source of news is a newspaper or possibly network TV	Your main source of news is CNN or possibly the Web.
You are most comfortable writing using a paper and pen and the written word.	You are most comfortable writing using a computer and the hyperword.

The MTR for the Information Age began in the 1960s with the advent of computers and television and the rise of institutional science in the U.S. The defining chasm in Newtonian versus Quantum thinking is between those who graduated from college prior to and after the 1970s. Those who graduated prior to 1970 can no more think in terms of Information-Age technologies than the sailing-ship Admirals who learned the ropes as Midshipmen on board ship in the 1840s could build pure steamships in the 1870s or the segregation-era Admirals who built their friendships in a totally white Navy of the 1920s could think integration in the 1950s. The class of 1975 is now just past fifty years old, which means that virtually all our senior leadership in the military and the IC is drawn from a generation that thinks computers are glorified typewriters and biology is about cutting up dead cats.

Projecting the process of the Information-Age reorientation in the IC, one can predict that RMA has not yet begun—mainly due to a lack of leadership comfortable in the Information-Age paradigm. One can project that the "Mahan" of the coming orientation revolution has not yet "written his book" (or more likely posted his website) because such a "Teacher" needs to be someone who could observe and reorient in a world dominated by Newtonian thinking but who "grew up" in the era of TV and computers. Cynthia Grabo and Col Boyd were almost there; they both observed and oriented in an Information-Age world dominated by Industrial-Age thinking; but neither were children of the Information Age.

Projecting from the sail-to-steam and segregation-to-integration revolutions in the Navy leads to a rather gloomy picture. The Information-Age MTR began in the 1960s, but the RMA is just beginning as young leadership—class of 1975 or later—who are younger than fifty, begin to build on the questioning started by forward-leaning analysts like Grabo and Boyd to orient and build a plan for reorienting the IC. Unfortunately, current attempts at integrating the IC by "solving the database problem" and building better analysis by building bigger and better satellites" bring to mind the era of the steam sloop or the era of an "integrated" Naval Academy that only graduates one or two Black Midshipman a year.

The completion of RMC for the Information-Age orientation revolution—with the advent of an equivalent indicator such as the "Great White Fleet" or the first Black Chief of Naval Operations—likely will not come for another two or three decades. That will require the rise of an Information-Age generation of leadership (currently still in college) who will be taught quantum thinking by the students of the Cynthia Grabo, Col Boyd, and other forward-leaning thinkers. Can we afford to wait that long?

Chapter 14

CAN WE SHIFT A PARADIGM IN A SINGLE GENERATION?

Potentially we can short-circuit the slow pace of the MTR-RMA-RMC progression to begin to build an Information-Age IC by beginning a program to capture the knowledge of senior analysts and to educate the rising analytical leadership to reorient the IC. But we must take step to do so now or the opportunity will be lost for at least another decade.

Potentially there exist things we can do *now* to short-circuit the slow pace of MTR-RMA-RMC progression. In my hypothesis for reorienting the IC, I indicated that it is much more important for the IC to build a pool of historians, librarians, and curators than to continue spending its budget on better technology such as new satellites and next-generation computers. Given that the current generation of leadership still thinks in the old Industrial-Age, "sailing ship" paradigm, it is unlikely that they will place an over-riding emphasis on fixing the broken Orientation step in the national OODA Cycle. Since they are ingrained with an over-riding emphasis on Action driven directly by Observation, the best we can hope for in at least the next decade is the equivalent of a "steam sloop"—where we will acknowledge the new paradigm without letting go of the old. The RMA will not come from the top down, but perhaps it can be hastened from the bottom up.

Lead, follow, or get the hell out of the way!
Old Navy Saying

The key to reorienting the IC is building a cadre of WMD and terrorism analysts who are subject-matter-experts on the history of their particular country or terrorist group as well as their particular WMD program, who routinely use MDA (or a more-developed successor) and who are comfortable doing analysis and production based on the hyperword. For convenience, I'll call these the First-Generation Reorienters. At this point in history, such analysts are virtually impossible to find. If we leave the process of training new ones to the natural changes in IC-wide leadership, it will take at least two generations. However, given a curious demographic distribution of analysts in the IC, there may be a way both to remember that history matters and to reorient to Information-Age thinking if we act very soon.

Demography is an historical discipline used by both biologists and political scientists to study populations and to predict the future characteristics of an animal or cultural population in terms of the age distribution of its members. While I have not yet directly incorporated demography into MDA, it is easy to do so because the standard demography chart looks like a chemist's Maxwell-Boltzmann curve and, therefore, like an organizational chart turned on its side. Age plotted on a demographic chart is a reflection of experience and skills so that the right-to-left demographic axis for a population approximates the bottom-to-top power axis on an organizational chart.

> Over the next 10 years approximately 50 percent of the technical experts in the Intelligence Community will retire. The junior analysts filling these positions (assuming the positions are filled, and not eliminated) may have the technical skills, but certainly will lack the experience and the issue-based knowledge of their predecessors. The mature Scientific and Technical Intelligence (S&TI) analyst is a dwindling species. Mastering the implications and subtle points of S&TI—and its significance for country and regional intelligence analysis—requires years of study and experience. Our lost S&TI analytical capability cannot be purchased quickly, nor for a limited period, and will literally take years to replace. While CW S&T shows a modest increase over the [1991-2001] period, biological warfare (BW) S&T resources decline—a surprising finding, considering its growing importance. [84]
>
> Scientific and Technical Intelligence Committee

We can get a glimpse of the future of the IC by charting its demographics. The key for the next decade is the curious bimodal distribution of analysts by age which follows from hiring practices over the last generation. During the Reagan administration military buildup, the IC expanded and hired many young analysts. Over the course of their careers, the career path was optimistic, leading to high retention. These are the IC's Senior Analysts, now in their 50s and early 60s, and they represent a significant portion of the IC's analytical assets. During the course of their careers, IC-wide hiring was low until the oldest analysts began to retire. Accordingly, today's IC has a bimodal distribution of analysts by age: Senior Analysts in their 50s and 60s and Junior Analysts in their late 20s and 30s with very few analysts in the 35- to 50-year-old range.

The Senior Analysts embody the IC's corporate knowledge with two or three decades' worth of experience as subject matter experts in their various fields. The

[84]Scientific and Technical Intelligence Committee, "The Health of Scientific and Technical Intelligence: A Study Conducted by the Scientific and Technical Intelligence Committee," (April 1998).

WMD analysts in this category have a wealth of knowledge on their target nations as well as on traditional S&T knowledge acquired prior to entering the IC. As such, they cannot be First-Generation Reorienters because they more likely have amassed their "shoeboxes" in paper, or at best MS Word files, and are not likely to be actively involved in database usage, open-source exploitation, or MDA. However, their knowledge, both what they know and what they have stored in their "shoeboxes," represents the historical baseline needed to start the MDA process.

On the other hand, the young analysts are children of the Information-Age and very computer and database savvy. From anecdotal observations of young BW analysts, I have noted that they can very rapidly use both classified and open-source databases to build a "shoebox" and electronic "3x5 card" deck if given senior analytical guidance, and are very interested in the IC's implementing new computer analytical tools for their use. As such they can become First-Generation Reorienters if they can be educated in the analytical art and can get access to an historical baseline required for MDA.

Strategic thinking and strategic planning go out to the next Decision Cycle. The most effective organization is one that can execute the current plan as rapidly and efficiently as possible ***while simultaneously rebuilding itself for a new plan***.

A First Step to Get There from Here

If the IC can change its emphasis from turning outward to handle customer taskers to turning inward to rebuild itself for the Information Age, there is a possible path to address the two major personnel challenges it faces—but by emphasizing "teachers" rather than "soldiers" to provide the leadership.

The first major challenge to reorient the IC in our lifetime is to capture the knowledge of the Senior Analysts. This requires two parts:

- Senior Analysts need to mentor young analysts to transition their tacit knowledge to the next generation. This will likely require hiring more analysts since many WMD accounts have only a single analyst assigned, and a Senior Analyst cannot mentor a young analyst on that WMD account unless the young analyst is available and not required on another account (where he or she has no senior analytical guidance), or is assigned to a "crisis support team."

The Changing Face of the IC

The curious demographics of the current IC are based on a large-scale hiring of analysts during the Reagan-era defense buildup with little replacement since then. This bimodal distribution means that the IC faces 2 major personnel challenges over the next decade.

1 *Senior Analysts* are retiring at an increasing rate. They are the "history" of the IC. Their knowledge must be captured both by mentoring the Rising Analytical Leadership and by archiving in "3x5 cards" in Entity databases.

2 *Rising Analytical Leadership* in the IC will come from the 35-45 year old analysts—old enough to start becoming "history" for the IC yet young enough to build the new kinds of databases for an Information-Age IC. These analysts are the IC's most precious asset for the future.

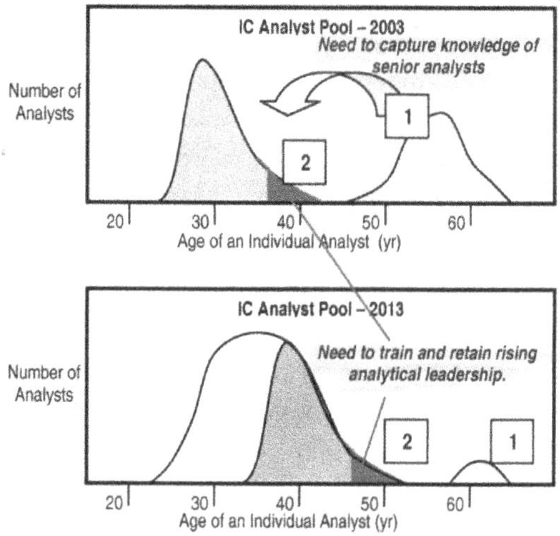

NOTE: distributions are idealized and not based on an actual census.

- The IC needs to hire enough IT and analytical support contractors to preserve the Senior Analysts' "shoeboxes" and extract the evidence from them into a standardized "entity database." Experience from several MDA experiments has indicated that tools to perform day-to-day WMD analysis of a target country are in place or can be very shortly in the pipeline, BUT turning the historical record from the printed word (or the printed word merely saved in electronic format) to hyperword is a daunting task that requires additional short-term help. A decade after the advent of the Internet in our current reorientation revolution, we are at the equivalent of a decade after Gutenberg printed his first Bible: printing any new books is straightforward as they are written; but it is only after we have gone back and printed versions of all the written books in the libraries that enough copies will be available to empower the "analysts" like Luther, and Newton, and Paine.

> The preservation of the historical record represented by the Senior Analysts' "shoeboxes" must be addressed *now* because any time a Senior Analyst retires and the young analyst who replaces him or her shreds all those documents (because they are merely on paper), a piece of our corporate knowledge is lost *forever.*

The second major challenge for reorienting the IC in our lifetime is empowering the Rising Analytical Leadership. By following the demographics of the IC, we can see that a decade in the future virtually all of today's Senior Analysts will have retired. Given the gap in longevity today, that means that over the next decade the mantle of "senior analyst" will rapidly move from analysts who are in their 50s today to analysts who in their 30s today, meaning that the IC's corporate knowledge is in for a huge drop—one that is already starting. Furthermore, there is *nothing* that we can do about it now because the gap in hiring over the last two decades cannot be repaired in any way. There is no academic or industrial pool of "analysts" like there is of lawyers or doctors that can be tapped to bring in experienced analysts; analysts must be trained from scratch by the IC. There is, however, a very small cadre of young analysts at the front edge of the demographic age curve who are the Rising Analytical Leadership for the Information-Age IC.

The Rising Analytical Leadership is a very small and very precious part of the IC: very small because there are few analysts who have entered the IC in the 1990s and have stayed for five to ten years to become leaders, and very precious because these are the only candidates to become First-Generation Orienters. These analysts are mature enough to understand the analytical process and have amassed a personal knowledge base both in their heads and in their "shoeboxes," yet young enough to be computer- and database-literate. These are the experts who will lead the IC into the Information Age.

Unfortunately, this is the very group that is being squeezed out of the IC by Industrial-Age personnel policies. There is no career pattern for the Rising Analytical Leadership. On one hand, they have hit a dead-end waiting for the Senior Analysts to retire because all the senior billets are already encumbered; on the other hand, they have begun to assume responsibilities well beyond their experience level due to the huge gap in leadership ahead of them. In addition, whenever there is a "database" problem to be addressed, it is those analysts who are tapped to solve it, not the Senior Analysts—who are considered database illiterates.

> Every member of the Rising Analytical Leadership—the GS-13s in their late 30s who are now the subject matter experts on WMD and terrorism accounts IC-wide—who leaves the IC due to lack of career advancement opportunities is a potential First-Generation Orienter who cannot be replaced for almost two more decades.

How Long Does it Take to Change a Culture? It Is Up to Us

A multidimensional analysis of the IC suggests both good news and bad news.

By learning the lessons of Cynthia Grabo and Col John Boyd we can begin to build methods and tools and reorient ourselves to provide strategic warning in an age of WMD and terrorism. Multidisciplinary Analysis (MDA) is a first-generation, Information-Age method that can serve as a basis for building better methods, and MS Word and PowerPoint are powerful tools that can serve as a basis for building better tools as long as we keep in mind that analysis is based on the research OODA Cycle which is commonly called hypothesis testing. Experiments in employing MDA on state-run WMD programs and terrorist CBRNE programs have shown that the methods, tools, and organizations are in place for Information-Age strategic analysis.

On the other hand, the major hurdle to an Information-Age IC is the realization that it is the Orientation step in the national OODA Cycle that is broken and that to implement Information-Age strategic analysis the IC needs to reorient itself from an emphasis on Observation-driven Action to an emphasis on Orientation-driven Decisionmaking. That reorientation requires quantum thinking and current IC leadership still operates on Newtonian thinking. This means that a top-down reorientation of the IC cannot begin for another generation when the current leadership retires and a new generation of senior leadership grows up that is comfortable with quantum models as outlined by Grabo and Boyd.

However, there is a possibility for bottom-up reorientation of the IC led by a cadre of Rising Analytical Leadership old enough to know that history matters, yet young enough to be comfortable with computers and databases. If we can empower that cadre to lead the reorientation of the IC, we can potentially skip a generation and start the process now. But if that cadre is lost, the IC will have to rebuild itself virtually from scratch, and will not have the expertise to do so for at least a decade.

SELECTED BIBLIOGRAPHY

Bodnar, John W. "How Long Does It Take to Change a Culture? Integration at the U.S. Naval Academy." *Armed Forces and Society* 25, no. 2 (Winter 1999): 289-306.

Boyd, Col John R. *A Discourse on Winning and Losing*. Collection of un-numbered briefing slides. August 1987.

Clark, Robert M. "Model Based Predictive Techniques." Lecture at the National Security Agency in 2001. (Available in: Robert M. Clark. *Intelligence Analysis*. CQ Press, 2003).

Grabo, Cynthia M. *Anticipating Surprise: Analysis for Strategic Warning*. Ed. Jan Goldman. Washington, DC: Joint Military Intelligence College's Center for Strategic Intelligence Research, 2002.

Kuhn, Thomas. *The Structure of Scientific Revolutions*. Chicago, IL: University of Chicago Press, 3rd edition, 1996.

Krygiel, Annette J. *Behind the Wizard's Curtain: An Integration Environment for a System of Systems*. Washington, DC: National Defense University, 1999.

Mahan, Alfred Thayer. *From Sail to Steam: Recollections of Naval Life.* New York: Harper & Brothers, 1907.

Rue, GySgt Steven S., USMC. *The Breakdown of the PC Paradigm: Information Display Technology As Analysis Inhibitor.* MSSI Thesis. Washington, DC: Joint Military Intelligence College, August 2003.

Scientific and Technical Intelligence Committee. "The Health of Scientific and Technical Intelligence: A Study Conducted by the Scientific and Technical Intelligence Committee." April 1998.

INDEX

D

E

F

G

H

I

J

K

L

M

N

O

P

R

S

T

U

W

ABOUT THE AUTHOR

John Bodnar has recently completed a year as a Research Fellow at the Joint Military Intelligence College on sabbatical from his position as a biological warfare analyst for the Defense Intelligence Agency. He served twenty-three years in the Navy in the submarine force and Naval Reserves. As a technology analyst in the Naval Reserves, CAPT Bodnar was associated with the Office of Naval Research and the Naval War College where he published several papers on the Revolution in Military Affairs. He completed a doctorate in biochemistry at Oregon State University and postdoctoral training in virology at Yale University. As a research biologist, Dr. Bodnar was a faculty member at Northeastern University and the U.S. Naval Academy and is currently an adjunct professor at Villa Julie College where he teaches bioinformatics. Dr Bodnar's biological research has included laboratory studies on viral growth and cellular structures as well as theoretical studies and computer simulations on the dynamics of gene networks in embryogenesis and organismal development. As a defense analyst, Dr. Bodnar has applied his network modeling approaches to several national and terrorist biological warfare programs and has provided analytical guidance to several research programs aimed at integrating computer technologies with analysis. The author may be contacted at JWBodnar70@hotmail.com or Bodnars@comcast.net.

Other Books from the Joint Military Intelligence College

Bodnar, John W. *Warning Analysis for the Information Age: Rethinking the Intelligence Process*, 2003.

Intelligence Professionalism in the Americas. Russell G. Swenson and Susana C. Lemozy, eds., 2003.

Bringing Intelligence About: Practitioners Reflect on Best Practices. Russell G. Swenson, ed., 2003.

Grabo, Cynthia M. *Anticipating Surprise: Analysis for Strategic Warning*. Jan Goldman, ed., 2002.

Clift, A. Denis. *Clift Notes*, 2nd Ed. James S. Major, ed., 2002.

Ensign, Eric S., LT, USCG. *Intelligence in the Rum War at Sea*, 1920-1933, 2001.

Clift, A. Denis. *Clift Notes*. James S. Major, ed., 2000.

Pickert, Perry L. *Intelligence for Multilateral Decision and Action*, 1997.

www.ingramcontent.com/pod-product-compliance
Lightning Source LLC
Chambersburg PA
CBHW080502110426
42742CB00017B/2978
9781782662518